MW01519084

Proverbs

Wisdom Builds God's House

Wisdom hath built her house ...
—Proverbs 9:1a

Proverbs

Wisdom Builds God's House

Stephen Kaung

Christian Fellowship Publishers, Inc.
New York

ISBN: 978-1-68062-096-2

Available from the Publishers at:

11515 Allecingie Parkway
Richmond, Virginia 23235
www.c-f-p.com

Printed in the United States of America

PREFACE

"Wisdom hath built her house, she hath hewn out her seven pillars" of support. So declared the book of Proverbs (9:1), whose author was Solomon, the wise King of Israel. Significantly, in this book's first part Solomon, as the above passage intimates, is found setting forth wisdom as personified; which is to say, that he presents wisdom as a living, active person. And given the symbolistic or typological connection between much of the Bible's Old Testament content and that of the New Testament, we are on solid ground to infer from this presentation that wisdom personified here is none other than God's Son, the Lord Jesus Christ.

Christ is the wisdom of God manifested from heaven on earth by the divine act of the Incarnation. And like Solomon of old who, through the wisdom granted to him from heaven, built the magnificent *physical* house of God—the temple in Jerusalem; just so, the "greater than Solomon"—even Christ himself (Matthew 12:42c ASV)—is today continuing to build God's *spiritual* house, which is the church, the body of Christ. And the material the Lord uses to build God's spiritual house is the sevenfold character of the Christ-life that is resident within every member of His church. And according to one's understanding of the book of Proverbs, the Seven Pillars of Wisdom alluded to in its chapter 9 can symbolically represent the seven different traits, attributes or features of Christ's noble character which can be found expressed throughout the many sayings appearing in this book of wisdom: Righteousness, Diligence, Love, Lowliness, Graciousness, Discipline, and Truthfulness.

Thus, Wisdom Personified seeks to progressively develop in us His followers these seven distinct traits of His character. And once He has established these in our lives, He shall be able to complete the building for His Father of that dwelling place of rest and peace which God has longed to have among His people. In order for this to be accomplished in us, however, we will need to submit ourselves to Christ totally and allow His Spirit who indwells us to develop and firmly establish these various character-traits in us so that Christ's virtuous character may be manifested through us as a testimony to the world and for touching those in need of moral and spiritual help. This is the Lord's purpose for us His people.

Hence, may we so give our lives over to Christ that the Holy Spirit shall have complete freedom to accomplish this in and through us. And thus, we shall be usable in the Lord's hands to fulfill God's will and purpose on the earth and bring Him much glory.

Contents

Publishers' Note

It should be noted that this series of messages was delivered by the author, as best as can be determined, sometime not long after the early part of 1964. They were delivered before a group of Christians who gathered together for worship in the New York City borough of Queens, USA. The texts of these messages were recorded and later transcribed for possible future publication. It should be further explained that in preparing these transcribed messages for today's publication, this entire book's text has been extensively edited and that numerous additional Scripture verses—both texts and/or citations thereof—have been inserted here and there where deemed necessary or helpful to the reader.

An Overview of the Book of Proverbs

Proverbs 1:1—Proverbs of Solomon, son of David, king of Israel.

This book in the Bible is a collection of proverbs. It is here called the "proverbs of Solomon." What is a proverb? It is usually a short sentence which conveys a moral truth in a concise and pointed manner. Which indicates that proverbs are usually fairly short, very concise, and very much to the point of what is desired to be conveyed. Sometimes a proverb is very clear and in other instances it may be very deep in meaning and therefore needing much meditation.

Proverbs—individually and collectively—are usually the result of a long history of meditations thereupon and the searchings of the ages. Generally speaking, a proverb cannot be traced to any one particular person. Such sayings are very much the product of the ages, they gradually having been developed, refined, and continually passed on from generation to generation. We do not know where a given proverb had its beginning, but we realize it must have had its initial creation sometime in the past. Indeed, every cultural group or nation has come to have its own collection of proverbs. They are the accumulation of that particular people's civilization.

Actually, the proverbs of the world's many nations and/or people groups have turned out to be quite similar. For instance, we who are Chinese have our proverbs in China and you here in America likewise have your proverbs; and yet, there are great similarities in both wording and meaning among them. Why is this the case? It is because in this universe there are basic moral and philosophical foundations underpinning all cultures, peoples, nations, and civilizations. Since all human beings come from one and the same source, the proverbs to be found among the world's different cultures, nations, and people groups are quite similar.

Whatever differences exist among these proverbs are due to the differences in background or environment of the peoples possessing their proverbs; whereas the basic truths and thoughts to be found in those peoples' and/or nations' proverbs are the same. Nevertheless, proverbs constitute national or cultural treasures; for they usually teach people how to live wisely and healthfully on this earth. And hence, they are very precious.

In contrast to proverbs, psalms are the expressions of the sentiments, feelings and emotions of the godly in their experience of God throughout their daily lives. In fact, the reading of the Bible's book of Psalms seem to help to lift the reader up to heaven and to be very close to God. Indeed, there is a certain spirituality to be gained from reading the book of Psalms. But in considering the book of Proverbs—whose contents are the maxims or wise sayings of this world—we may at first think that such maxims and sayings are very earthbound in nature and are therefore lacking in spirituality. In our considering the matter more deeply, however, it is my belief that if a believer lives very close to God and truly enters into the feelings and sentiments being expressed by the various psalmists, that believer will most certainly live before both God and man in this world by means of the wisdom to be found in the book of Proverbs. In other words, the content of Proverbs presents the practical side of our Christian life: how we should live wisely on this earth before man—and yes, also before God (cf. Ezekiel 33:10c). And there is therefore a spirituality to be gained by adopting in one's Christian life and walk the many wise sayings and counsels which fill the book of Proverbs.

The Proverbs of the Bible

Now there is a great difference between the proverbs in the Bible and those of the nations and peoples of this world.

Wisdom Founded upon God

The proverbs in this Bible book are founded upon God. In other words, God himself is the foundation of all these Biblical proverbs, whereas the proverbs of the nations are not founded on

God but are solely the wise sayings of man: though they may be witty, clever, and often quite serious meditations on the various experiences of men throughout the ages, they are nonetheless human expressions without God and His involvement at all. The Bible's proverbs, however, all have God as their foundation; they not only teach man how to live wisely, but how, according to God, to live wisely before man's fellow human beings.

Wisdom from Above

These Biblical proverbs are attributed in their very text to King Solomon: "Proverbs of Solomon." We do not know whether he was the one who collected these proverbs or improved or refined them; or whether he spoke these particular proverbs from himself. It might have been both. Either way, we know that Solomon spoke 3000 proverbs (I Kings 4:32a), and the whole book of Proverbs contains only some 600 verses, thus numbering only about a quarter of what Solomon had spoken.

King Solomon is considered in Scripture as being a symbol of wisdom. And the basis for that is as follows. When Solomon ascended to Israel's throne he went to Gibeon to offer to God because he greatly loved Him. God then appeared to him in a dream in the night and asked him what he wanted. Solomon prayed and said, "Lord, I am but a little child. I do not know how to judge Your people. I do not know how to go in and out before this great people of Yours. Therefore, give me understanding; grant me wisdom; that is what I need most of all, so that I may judge Your people according to You yourself" (see I Kings 3:4-15, II Chronicles 1:2-12).

God was greatly pleased with Solomon's demeanor and his request. For the Bible says that God gave him great wisdom, understanding of heart, largeness of heart, a hearing heart, a heart that could hear the voice of God; and thus his wisdom excelled all the wisdom of the sons of the East. It excelled all the wisdom of Egypt. His wisdom excelled even that of wise men such as Ethan, Heman, Calcol, and Darda. In fact, his wisdom excelled that of everybody (I Kings 4:29-31).

We can see from this Biblical account of what happened that Solomon's wisdom was that of another kind—that his wisdom was of a much higher standard than the best wisdom of this world. In other words, it could rightly be said that Solomon's wisdom came from above, that it came from God himself. Solomon could see things with the eyes of God: he could hear God's voice—God's messages—in all things. It can therefore be concluded that the Bible's book of Proverbs is unique, in that its wisdom is not the wisdom from beneath but is the "wisdom from above" (James 3:17a). And thus, having God as its very foundation, the book of Proverbs can teach us how, according to God, we are to walk wisely on the earth. How very practical is this Bible book of wisdom, and I do believe that we are much in need of such wisdom.

Wisdom Personified

This book of Scripture is a collection of many, many proverbs, and every one of them is precious. Each of us needs to read them one by one, then take and implement, literally, every one of them in our lives. That is a spiritual exercise which all of us can do ourselves. What I wish to do in our covering this book together is that which is more general in nature. And to that end, we at the outset must acknowledge together that there is One who is much greater than even Solomon in all his wisdom and glory (Matthew 12:42c). Yes, we have here before us all the wise proverbs given to us from the wisest person to have lived in all the ages of mankind's history; and yet, we have been given to see in Scripture and from that One's own lips that there is One greater than even wise King Solomon. And hence, it is my hope that by reviewing together these many wise sayings of Solomon we may hear the voice of the One who is far, far greater than Solomon—even God's Son, the Lord Jesus Christ.

Solomon spoke great wisdom by means of his proverbs. Yet what—or more correctly who—is the wisdom that Solomon was speaking about? For we learn from the book of Proverbs itself that wisdom has been represented to its readers in terms of personification; which is to say, that wisdom has not been portrayed by Solomon as merely an abstract idea such as it being a skill or an ability. To the contrary, Solomon is found imputing personality to wisdom. In other words, wisdom has been put forth here as a person, and that person is none other than the Lord Jesus himself. We thus understand that Solomon was speaking forth about wisdom personified. And we who have believed in Him who is Wisdom incarnate can thank God that because we have the Lord Jesus in us as our very life (Colossians 3:4a; cf. Philippians 1:21a), we have Christ as our very wisdom, since God has made Him so to us (I Corinthians 1:30b).

It is important for us to realize that though the book of Proverbs is indeed a volume of ethics—even *Christian* ethics, it is not to be construed as a book of rules and regulations which instruct us outwardly on what the believer in Christ should do and what the believer should not do. Moreover, the book is not to be approached as containing that which the Christian must try to remember and do as a means by which to improve oneself. Not so on both counts. Instead, we as Christians must recognize the fact that the Wisdom of whom Proverbs speaks—even Christ himself—resides within us, and that as we walk in union with Him by following Him as His disciples, then the reality of all these maxims, sayings and truths in this book full of wisdom shall practically flow out from that life of wisdom resident within us.

To describe the matter another way, our approach as Christians to this book of wise sayings is not to view it as a self-improvement program full of "do's" and "don'ts" on how to live out the Christian life but to recognize that by cooperating with the Wisdom-life within us, the content of Proverbs will come forth quite naturally from within. Such is the difference between morality and spirituality, between the ethics of this world and Christian ethics.

The former is founded upon the rules and laws which are outside of us and which we outwardly cultivate and attempt to do them all by ourselves. On the other hand, Christian ethics is founded upon the fact that God has first given us the Wisdom-life by which to now live as believers in Christ, and that by cooperating with that Wisdom-life—even Christ's life—resident within us, all those commendable outward actions called for in the book of Proverbs will supernaturally outflow naturally from within us. And that can be termed spirituality in contradistinction to morality.

Wisdom on Practical Living

Proverbs is a book of wisdom on practical living. And we can correctly characterize Jesus' so-called Sermon on the Mount as being of the same category (Matthew 5-7), in that the One who is greater than Solomon is telling us certain practical things. Moreover, in reviewing the practical sections of all the New Testament epistles we shall discover that they, too, are of the same character as that of Proverbs and Christ's lengthy so-called sermon. Furthermore, all these segments of Scripture point up the very important fact that our Christian life is two-dimensional: that it possesses not only the vertical aspect—the life with God—and which is particularly laid out for us in the book of Psalms, but it also possesses the horizontal dimension—our life before the watching world—and which we find delineated for us in the book of Proverbs. All this is simply another way of saying that on the one hand God grants us His divine life by gifting us with the Christ-life within; and then out of that life there flows forth from us His life in terms of our practical daily experience. And such will serve as a strong testimony to God.

Hence, I very much hope that we shall come to realize the importance of the book of Proverbs, and that the expression of our practical life on earth must be an outflow of the Christ-life within so that we may bear a truly living testimony to the Lord Jesus. And I firmly believe that a study on Proverbs can aid us greatly in that regard.

An Outline of Proverbs

Now the entire book of Proverbs can be divided very roughly into three parts. The first part, which I have chosen to entitle,

Wisdom Calls, consists of the book's first nine chapters; and they together serve as an introduction. As we shall shortly see, Wisdom Personified—God's beloved Son—is calling us to himself. This initial part of the book is therefore introductory in nature.

The book's middle section runs from chapter 10 through chapter 24. This second part consists of *the* proverbs of Solomon: there are a total of 375 wise sayings to be found in this part of the book. And I have suggested this section's title as, Wisdom Builds. If Solomon's proverbs can be described as "wisdom instructs" or as "wisdom flows forth," then it can rightly be said that as a result "wisdom builds" character.

It needs to be pointed out further that in reading this second part carefully we shall notice that within its contents—from chapter 22:17 through chapter 24:34—there is a collection of sayings whose opening words of invitation reads as follows: "Incline thine ear, and hear the words of the wise." These were not the proverbs of Solomon; and though we do not know for certain who these wise men were, it is thought that probably they were those who stood in service before King Solomon. In standing before fallen mankind's wisest man, one is bound to become wise, too. Part Two, then, contains the wise words of Solomon and also those of certain other wise men of that period.

The concluding section of Proverbs, Part Three, consists of two distinct segments which together form the content of chapters 25 through 31. These seven concluding chapters to the book of Proverbs have together been characterized as "wisdom continues to instruct" or "wisdom overflows" or "wisdom beautifies." I have selected the third of these characterizations as the overall title I have given to this final portion of the book. And the proverbs and maxims to be found here are: (a) those additional wise sayings collected by good King Hezekiah some 200 years later and which are found in chapters 25 to 29; and (b) the many wise words of two unusual people—the man Agur and the Queen Mother of Massa—both of whom belonged to the community of Massa, the home village of an Arabian desert tribe of Ishmaelites. Their wise words are to be found in the very last two chapters of

Proverbs (30-31) and serve as an appendix of sorts to this concluding Part Three of the book.

By way of closing our time today in beginning to consider together the book of Proverbs, I believe it would be very profitable for us if we would seriously study this precious portion of Scripture. Martin Luther once suggested that Christians should use Proverbs as a devotional book. Especially do I believe this would be good for the young people among us to do. We all should read it, study it, and even memorize portions of it until its wisdom becomes an essential part of our daily life. Such a spiritual undertaking will teach us how to live and walk upon this earth rightly. Hence, if you feel you need wisdom, read and study the book of Proverbs.

PART ONE

Wisdom Calls (Chapters 1-9)

"Doth not wisdom cry? and understanding give forth
her voice? ... Unto you, men, I call ..."

Proverbs 8:1, 4a

The first nine chapters of Proverbs serve as an introduction to the rest of this Bible book's contents. And in this introduction wisdom is presented as calling us to come to her, to seek her above all things and to treasure her above gold and silver. And if we respond to her call in that manner, we shall be greatly blessed.

As intimated earlier, Wisdom Personified in the book of Proverbs is actually none other than the Lord Jesus Christ; and He is calling us to himself. He is calling us His followers to sit down with Him in fellowship at His table, to feed upon Him and enjoy Him. And if we do this, we shall live on this earth with wisdom and strength.

> Proverbs 1:1-6—Proverbs of Solomon, son of David, king of Israel: To know wisdom and instruction; to discern the words of understanding; to receive the instruction of wisdom, righteousness and judgment, and equity; to give prudence to the simple, to the young man knowledge and discretion. He that is wise will hear, and will increase learning; and the intelligent will gain wise counsels: to understand a proverb and an allegory, the words of the wise and their enigmas.

From this opening passage to the entire book we are given to see the purpose of Proverbs: What will these proverbs do for us? To whom are these wise sayings given and therefore who will be helped by them?

What These Proverbs Can Provide

Altogether there are twelve different skills for living rightly which these many and varied proverbs in this Bible book can give or provide to us and which are very practical in nature in enabling us believers to walk before God in a satisfactory manner. These skills or abilities, which are referenced in the above-quoted opening passage of Proverbs, are as follows.

1. To know wisdom. The word wisdom which appears in the opening verse of Proverbs has a root form in the Hebrew language meaning skillful or practical. Thus, wisdom is different in meaning from that of knowledge. Whereas knowledge is facts, data, or information about this or that which a person may gather or accumulate, wisdom is the skill or ability to make wise use of that accumulated knowledge. Another way of distinguishing between the two terms can be summed up this way: How a person applies the knowledge he has to a given situation, challenge or problem, and does so wisely—that is wisdom. And hence, it can be asserted that proverbs afford a person the skill or ability to practically use the knowledge gained, collected, or accumulated—and do so wisely and correctly.

2. To know instruction. The word instruction appearing here not only has reference to instructing or teaching but also includes the thought of correction, discipline and warning. As used here the word instruction is therefore not meant to convey an abstract philosophical idea. We are not only to know the various proper morals or ethics in our lives but also the discipline connected with maintaining the proper standards. There are very real disciplines, corrections and warnings which have their place in our lives.

3. To discern the words of understanding. Discernment is very important in our Christian life. Unfortunately, one of the problems among believers today is their lack of spiritual discernment in being able to know—to distinguish—the difference between things; and as a sad consequence, they do not know how to rightly walk and live out the Christian life. If, for example, we cannot discern the difference between right and wrong, good and evil, what is of life and what is of death, then we are lost. We need spiritual discernment, and as this opening passage of Proverbs implies, we are not merely to hear God's word but we are also to discern the words of understanding.

In Paul's prayer for the Philippian believers this apostle uttered the following:

... this I pray, that your love may abound more and more in knowledge and all discernment; so that ye may distinguish between the things that differ; that ye may be sincere [or, pure—Darby] and void of offence unto the day of Christ (1:9-10 ASV mgn).

Oh, that we may have an understanding heart, that we may discern the words of understanding. And proverbs—those wise sayings from heaven given to Solomon—can provide us with this kind of spiritual discernment in our daily life.

4. To receive the instruction of wisdom. This Darby translation of the descriptive phrase of this fourth aspect of what a proverb can provide can be stated differently: "To receive the *discipline* of wisdom." Moreover, in the original Hebrew the word translated here as wisdom is different from the other and more often used word in Proverbs that is translated in English as wisdom. For here in this phrase the word translated as wisdom actually means: to be intelligent, to know the essence of something. And hence, a more completely accurate rendering in English of this phrase would be: "To receive the discipline of intelligence."

5. Righteousness. Or: Integrity, Goodness.

6. Judgment. Or: To live justly.

7. Equity. Or: To live fairly.

8. Prudence. What is prudence? In the original Hebrew this word means "smoothness"; "the capacity to escape the viles of evil." Because, explained Jesus to His disciples, they would be "as sheep in the midst of wolves" when sent forth in ministry, therefore, He added, "be prudent as the serpents, and guileless as the doves" (Matthew 10:16). We, too, need prudence in our day if we are going to be able to serve God wisely.

9. Knowledge.

10. Discretion. This word means "thoughtfulness, careful thinking." In other words, this conveys the thought of reflection.

11. Learning.

12. Counsels.

These, then, are the various abilities which Christians will begin to have in their lives as the result of their learning and implementing the proverbs in this book of Scripture. Indeed, these twelve skills are very important and necessary for living wisely and practically on this earth.

To Whom the Proverbs Are Given

And to whom are the proverbs given? Who will be profited by them? Once again, they are identified within this same opening passage to the book of Proverbs, as follows.

1. *"To give prudence to the simple."* The word simple here has reference to those who are ignorant. When reading Proverbs those who are ignorant will begin to gain prudence and thus they shall become wise.

2. *"To the young man, knowledge and discretion."* From this passage we can infer that proverbs are especially beneficial for young believers. I would certainly urge them to read this book of numerous helpful wise sayings, for such will make younger Christians wise in that these proverbs will give them "knowledge" and grant them "discretion"—that is, reflection or sagacity. And thus, young believers will not be superficial but will have depth in their knowledge and discretion and will accordingly not act impulsively.

If I may say so, generally speaking, younger Christians have a problem, in that they too often act impulsively, rashly, instantly without carefully thinking through a given situation, problem or challenge with which they are confronted in their lives. The taking to heart of these proverbs, however, can provide them with the prudent ability to act according to deeper and therefore careful thinking which is based upon true knowledge, rather than to act hastily or utter words impulsively without any thought whatsoever.

Such, it may be pointed out, constitute some important purposes proverbs can fulfill in the lives of believers—especially in the lives of young believers.

3. *"He that is wise will hear."* Not only are these proverbs given for the simple (of course they need it); not only are they for the young people (we have just now realized that they need them as

well); but also they are given for the wise. If you think you are wise and highly intelligent, then you need to take to yourself these proverbs to make you even wiser! Proverbs are therefore useful for everybody. We all need them.

Several Important Themes Related to Wisdom

Several important themes related to God's wisdom are to be found in these first nine chapters of Proverbs. There are four in particular which I believe need to be mentioned and discussed to some extent.

The Fear of the Lord and the Love of God

"The fear of Jehovah is the beginning of knowledge" (Proverbs 1:7).

"The fear of Jehovah is the beginning of wisdom; and the knowledge of the Holy [or, of holy things] is intelligence" (Proverbs 9:10).

"Then shalt thou understand the fear of Jehovah, and find the knowledge of God. For Jehovah giveth wisdom; out of His mouth come knowledge and understanding" (Proverbs 2:5-6).

The fear of the Lord is the beginning of wisdom and of knowledge. In Old Testament times the highest spiritual achievement a person could arrive at was to fear the Lord. If a person should fear the Lord, that was considered as being the beginning of knowledge and the beginning of wisdom. In our New Testament era the highest spiritual fulfillment that a person can arrive at is the possession of the love of God. Why so with respect to God's love? Simply because Christ has already come and has given us His own life; therefore, the highest achievement a person can arrive at spiritually is to love God.

Nevertheless, though that is all true, I believe there is a misunderstanding about the relationship between the love of God and this matter of fear. Some Christians think that if there is the love of God then there can be no fear of any kind present, for they proceed to quote I John 4 which states that "perfect love casts out fear" (v. 18b). That statement, of course, is true; but let us understand that the fear cited in this verse has reference to the fear of punishment: that if there is perfect love towards God, a person need not fear of being punished: that that kind of fear is gone. Please realize, however, that even in love there is the element of fear: yet not the fear of being punished but the fear of displeasing the one whom you love. *That* kind of fear is always present in perfect love. And that fear is of a holy kind when applying this truth to the Christian's perfect love towards God. Furthermore, if the element of fear of the kind just now described is missing in love—whether that be love towards a fellow human or towards God—then it can be said that that one's love is not perfect.

Now as the verses quoted above from Proverbs chapters 1, 9 and 2 intimate, the fear of the Lord is the beginning of possessing divine knowledge and wisdom. And hence, if a person does not fear God—that is, if a person is not afraid of displeasing God—then that one has no heavenly knowledge and wisdom. You may be very intelligent, have learned much, and thus have come to know much *about* things of heaven and earth; yet all that knowledge and wisdom acquired are solely from beneath and not the knowledge and wisdom which comes from above. What you have gained is not heavenly knowledge and wisdom but only the earthly. Indeed, you have not even *begun* to acquire the wisdom and knowledge from above.

Oh how we need to learn to fear God! We need to learn to be fearful lest somehow we displease Him. There should always be that desire within us that because we love Him, we want to please Him. And as we gain this strong desire within us, there shall be a holy fear present. Such will be spiritually very healthy, and the result shall be that we will begin to have heavenly knowledge and wisdom.

Consider for a moment Joseph back in Old Testament times. Because he feared God there came to him great wisdom from above. Not only was he delivered from evil and delivered from falling into temptation, he was also granted the ability to interpret dreams and to rule wisely over Egypt as the second most powerful authority in the land. So let us, too, cultivate having a holy fear. Let us not harbor a fear of punishment but, because we love God, we do not want to displease Him.

Now as was noted earlier, wisdom in the opening chapters of Proverbs is personified, and such is none other than God's beloved Son the Lord Jesus Christ. And one of the central characteristics of the life of Christ is this holy fear of which I have been speaking. For in the Old Testament prophetic book of Isaiah it was prophesied concerning the coming Messiah—even Jesus— that the Spirit of Jehovah God shall rest upon Him (11:2a). And as was presented in that prophecy, one of the sevenfold descriptions of the Spirit resting upon Him was "the fear of Jehovah" (11:1-2). Indeed, this very trait in the earthly life of the Lord Jesus has been fully borne out in all four Gospel narratives in the New Testament describing His walk on earth before God His Father; namely, that there was always that holy fear of displeasing the Father.

Oh, Jesus said and did all things to please His Father, He not wishing to say or do anything which in any way might displease Him. And according to Proverbs that holy fear is wisdom. And that aspect of the Spirit of Jehovah upon Christ figured centrally in the life of Jesus, for in the same prophecy in Isaiah concerning Messiah-Jesus, it further declares that "his delight will be in the fear of Jehovah" (v. 3a). Accordingly, because of our having the life of Christ in us, there should be this same strong desire within us of the fear of the Lord; and that shall be the beginning of wisdom for us.

The Qualities of Wisdom Personified

A second theme related to God's wisdom revolves around the qualities of that wisdom. We may therefore inquire: What are the qualities or attributes of Wisdom Personified? A passage in Proverbs chapter 8 recounts them for us:

I wisdom dwell with prudence, and find the knowledge which cometh of reflection. The fear of Jehovah is to hate evil; pride, and arrogancy, and the evil way, and the froward mouth do I hate. Counsel is mine, and sound wisdom: I am intelligence; I have strength. By me kings reign, and rulers make just decrees; by me princes rule, and nobles, all the judges of the earth (vv. 12-16).

This passage reveals the sevenfold qualities of Wisdom Personified. Christ as Wisdom Personified is prudent; He engages in reflection; He has a fear of Jehovah God that hates all forms of evil; He is able to provide counsel; He possesses sound wisdom (that is, sanctified common sense); He is a deep source of intelligence; and He has inexhaustible strength.

These qualities or attributes of Wisdom are all so precious that we shall seek after Him more than questing after silver and gold, because He is the most precious possession that we can ever obtain in this world.

A Third Theme: What Wisdom Personified Provides Us

"Turn you at my reproof: behold, I will pour forth my spirit upon you, I will make known to you my words" (Proverbs 1:23).If we listen to Wisdom, He will pour His Spirit upon us.

"… whoso hearkeneth unto me shall dwell safely, and shall be at rest from fear of evil" (Proverbs 1:33). The acquiring of Him who is divine wisdom will grant us protection, deliver us from fear, and provide us with peace and rest.

"… discretion shall keep thee, understanding shall preserve thee: to deliver thee from the way of evil, from the man that speakest froward things; from those who leave the paths of uprightness, to walk in the ways of darkness …" (Proverbs 2:11-13). Wisdom gained will deliver us, and preserve us.

"… length of days, and years of life, and peace shall they [i.e., Wisdom's law and commandments] add to thee (Proverbs 3:2) … they [Wisdom's words and sayings] are life unto those that find them, and health to all their flesh" (Proverbs 4:22). Heavenly wisdom's words and sayings, His law and commandments, are life, length of days, health, and peace to us.

"… that I may cause those that love me to inherit substance; and I will fill their treasuries" (Proverbs 8:21). In other words, we will be filled with heavenly treasures because we love Him who is Wisdom.

A Fourth Theme: What Our Response towards Wisdom Personified Is to Be

"My son, if thou receivest my words, and layeth up my commandments with thee, so that thou incline thine ear unto wisdom, and thou apply thy heart to understanding; yea, if thou criest after discernment, and liftest up thy voice to understanding; if thou seekest her as silver, and searchest for her as for hidden treasures" (Proverbs 2:1-4). Oh how we need to seek for Him who is Wisdom as being the most precious possession in life we could ever obtain.

"Let not loving-kindness and truth forsake thee; bind them about thy neck, write them upon the tablet of thy heart" (Proverbs 3:3). This is the way we should respond to Wisdom Personified: that we should bind these wise words of His upon our necks and have them written upon our hearts.

"My son, attend to my words; incline thine ear unto my sayings" (Proverbs 4:20). How we need to incline our ears to Wisdom's sayings and to pay attention to His words; and that shall be the right response on our part towards Him who is Wisdom. As has repeatedly been made quite clear, this Wisdom is Christ himself, and because He is in us, He is our wisdom. How we need, therefore, to seek after Him! How we need to hear Him! How we need to treasure Him! If we do, then in our daily walk we will live wisely towards man and before man according to God. And that shall be our good testimony.

Our heavenly Father, how we praise and thank Thee, that the wisdom which is from above is nothing abstract; that wisdom is indeed Christ our Lord himself.

Oh, how we praise and thank Thee that Thou hast made Christ our wisdom, righteousness, sanctification, and redemption. We do find our all in Him, and for this we are most thankful. We pray that we may have a right attitude towards wisdom, even towards Christ himself. Oh, that we may seek Him, that we may incline our ears and our hearts towards Him—so that we may walk wisely on this earth. Father, do help us to make all these matters very practical in our daily lives and that it may all be to Thy praise and glory. We ask in the name of our Lord Jesus. Amen.

PART TWO

Wisdom Builds (Chapters 10-24)

Wisdom hath built her house, she hath
hewn out her seven pillars ...
Proverbs 9:1

Introduction:

Wisdom's House and Its Seven Pillars

We shall now proceed to consider more specifically the second part of Proverbs. The proverbs to be found here are those of Solomon. As was noted earlier Proverbs' first nine chapters serve as an introduction to all the rest of this book of sayings and maxims. For the most part those initial chapters were marked by lengthy exhortations. Here in this Part Two, though, we come upon *real* proverbs, for the latter are usually very short statements which convey moral truths in a concise and pointed manner. And hence, in looking into chapter 10 and on through to chapter 24, proverbs—that is, short pithy sayings—are to be seen everywhere throughout these many chapters.

Now there is a superscription that appears above the opening of chapter 10 which declares that what follows are "The Proverbs of Solomon." We have been told elsewhere in the Old Testament Scriptures (I Kings 4:32a) that King Solomon had spoken 3000 proverbs. In this Part Two of the book of Proverbs, however, we find only a limited portion of those 3000. Most likely they were either spoken by Solomon or else they were collected together by him and improved upon by him. In fact, all these proverbs bear the mark of Solomonic wisdom.

Every proverb in this collection of Solomon's sayings is worth more than gold. It would be good if we could weigh each proverb to be found here; but at least we should meditate on each and all of them, reflect deeply upon them, and look to the Lord concerning them. In that way God's word may truly sink deeply into our very being.

To repeat, it would be good and most profitable if we would ponder and dwell upon these proverbs before the Lord. My purpose, though, in our considering this book of Scripture during the remaining times of our fellowship together will not permit us to do that; otherwise, we could spend the rest of our years contemplating and meditating upon these many proverbs. Instead, my purpose in delving into this book with you will be to gather up all the proverbs included in its pages and attempt to discover some essential truths which are to be practically implemented in our spiritual lives. And as an aid in accomplishing this purpose I would like to borrow a metaphor from the book of Proverbs itself.

The House of God

"Wisdom hath built her house, she hath hewn out her seven pillars … " (Proverbs 9:1). Wisdom has built her house and she has hewn out seven pillars. You do not need wisdom to destroy, but you do need wisdom to build. Solomon was a man of much wisdom, and therefore he could be a *great* builder. His one great work was that he built the House of God—the Jerusalem Temple. He built that temple with massive stones—in fact, three layers of them. He overlaid them with wood and with pure gold. He also hewed out two gigantic pillars which stood before the House of God as a testimony (I Kings 7:15-22). In short, King Solomon, as the man of much wisdom, built to the glory of God. Indeed, he constructed a temple-house upon which God could, and did, put His name (I Kings 9:3b).

Now we who are followers of Christ have One greater than Solomon with us, even the Lord Jesus Christ (Matthew 12:42c, Luke 11:31c). He is far greater than Solomon because He is Wisdom itself. And surely the Lord Jesus is building God's house yet today.

In this very connection, let us remind ourselves that the Lord Jesus declared: "I will build my church upon this rock, and the gates of Hades shall not prevail against it" (see Matthew 16:18b). The Lord is Wisdom incarnate, and He is building God's house which is the church. Jesus, of course, is the very foundation of God's house, the church; but exactly with what materials does He build? He builds with us who have believed in Him. Yet in what way does He build with us? Well, at first, the Lord Jesus engages in developing and maturing certain character-traits in us, and as

He is establishing those traits in us, or, to describe it somewhat differently, as He is developing *His* character in us as *our* character, then He is able, with us as His acceptable construction materials, to build a house that is fit for God the Father to dwell in.

Even though we believers in Christ have been put together as the church and house of God, if there is not the work of Christ progressively taking place in us by the Holy Spirit in terms of character-building, we shall never constitute a house that is fit to be God's dwelling place. What is therefore necessary is for Christ to have developed in us His very self: which is the kind of character that is heavenly in nature and not earthly. In other words, Christ's character has to distinguish us from that of fallen Adam. And with the Lord's various attributes of character established in us, He by the Spirit can build us into a dwelling place which is most suitable for God to rest in in peace.

Now we are rightly considering together here the matter of the *development* of character, since character itself is not that which is brought into being in us humans at our birth. To the contrary, character has to be developed. Yes, we are born with a nature, but only when that nature is developed can it be said that there emerges what is called character. We are told in II Peter that God by His divine power has given us all things relating to life and godliness (1:3). Indeed, God has given us His very own Son, and along with His Son His life automatically becomes resident within us by His Spirit. And that life has within it its own nature which is heavenly; which means that there is a potentiality in us to become like Christ in His very character.

This divine-character potentiality, however, has to be developed, increased and matured in us if Christ's character is going to characterize our spiritual life. For though we who have believed in Christ have His very life that is possessed of its own divine nature, if we do not follow and cooperate with that nature, we shall not have the character of Christ in us in its various traits or attributes. Hence, if we fail to provide opportunity for the divine nature of Christ's life to be progressively established in us, then that nature cannot manifest itself in and through us in the form of Christ's various character-traits. If, though, Christians have cooperated with the development of that heavenly nature in themselves, there shall come forth the aforementioned traits of character; and in our considering the combination of all such traits together, what we see emerging in those Christians is a well-rounded and praiseworthy personality, and that personality is none other than Christ himself.

What has just now been described is what we find expressed in the Bible. In fact, this is what one particular Scripture passage means in stating that we "are progressively being transformed into [Christ's] image from one degree of glory to even more glory ..." (II Corinthians 3:18b Amplified). We can thus discern from this passage that this is not merely some teaching having something to do with the believer externally, but that it has everything to do with the Christian internally: the development, growth and maturation of inward character: that all which characterizes Christ shall characterize us who cooperate with the Lord. And hence, those who possess Christ's character become the materials with which the Lord is able to build a spiritual house and home on earth wherein God can take up His abode and rest in peace.

The Seven Pillars of Wisdom

"Wisdom hath built her house, she hath hewn out her seven pillars ... " (Proverbs 9:1). This is a house whose construction included the presence and support of seven huge pillars, thus indicating that *this* edifice is *well* supported. Furthermore, this feature is indicative of the fact that the building of this particular house was not a hurried undertaking whose construction was carried out without there being support sufficient enough to withstand whatever fierce winds and raging flood waters might come; otherwise, the house would collapse. No, Wisdom has built her house with the inclusion of seven strong pillars. And as stated earlier, I wish to borrow this metaphor as we continue to fellowship together concerning this book of Proverbs.

Now, of course, we would like to know what these pillars might represent. I believe we can say that, in line with all which has been shared thus far regarding this book of Proverbs, these seven pillars can be viewed symbolically as seven distinct traits of character. Wisdom Personified, even the Lord Jesus Christ, is working to progressively develop in us His followers seven different traits, attributes or aspects of character. And once He has established these in our lives, He is able to build for God that dwelling place of rest and peace He has longed to have among His people.

I need to point out, however, that instead of our looking into each one of the relevant proverbs, maxims or sayings individually, I would like to group together into seven different pillars, so to speak, all of those proverbs which are related to each of the seven different character-traits. And these seven different Wisdom pillars, representing as they do symbolically seven distinct attributes or traits of character—both positively stated and their negative opposites shown—are as follows:

1. Righteousness (Integrity, Goodness) vs. Wickedness
2. Diligence vs. Slothfulness
3. Love vs. Hate
4. Lowliness (Humility) vs. Pride (Haughtiness)
5. Graciousness (Mercifulness, Gentleness, Liberality)
                    vs. Cruelty (Anger, Violence)
6. Discipline (Prudence) vs. Foolishness (Simplemindedness)
7. Truthfulness (Honesty, Faithfulness) vs. Lying (Hypocrisy)

These seven different character-traits, which are spread forth throughout the entire book of Proverbs, are repeated over and over many, many times. And each grouping of related proverbs or sayings representing each one of these traits of character we shall view and consider as being one of the seven pillars that Wisdom Personified shall have hewn out and which He shall use to support the House of God's Rest that He is building.

Pillar 1—The Character-Trait of Righteousness

Proverbs 10:2—Treasures of wickedness profit nothing; but righteousness delivereth from death.

Proverbs 10:3—Jehovah suffereth not the soul of the righteous man to famish; but he repelleth the craving of the wicked.

Proverbs 10:6—Blessings are upon the head of a righteous man; but the mouth of the wicked covereth violence.

Proverbs 10:11—The mouth of a righteous man is a fountain of life; but the mouth of the wicked covereth violence.

Proverbs 10:16—The labour of a righteous man tendeth to life; the revenue of a wicked man, to sin.

Proverbs 10:20—The tongue of the righteous man is as choice silver; the heart of the wicked is little worth.

Proverbs 10:21—The lips of a righteous man feed many; but fools die for want of understanding .

Proverbs 10:30—The righteous man shall never be moved; but the wicked shall not inhabit the land.

Proverbs 10:31—The mouth of a righteous man putteth forth wisdom; but the froward tongue shall be cut out.

Proverbs 10:32—The lips of a righteous man know what is acceptable; but the mouth of the wicked is frowardness.

In the book of Proverbs one can find the word righteous used either as an adjective or as a noun. It is repeated throughout the book too many times to list them all, so I have listed some here from only chapter 10 to provide some examples.

Christ Our Righteousness

Our Position before God

Before we believed in the Lord Jesus, what was the one thing which characterized us? Sin. Sin is the opposite of righteousness: it is *un*righteousness. That is the one thing which still characterizes fallen mankind. Before believing in Jesus we had no righteousness. We thought we had some, but those righteousnesses of ours were as filthy rags in the sight of God (Isaiah 64:6a). There is none righteous, not even one (Romans 3:10); and the wages of sin is death (6:23a). That was our condition, our state—even our very character. Not only us, but sin and unrighteousness characterizes all of fallen mankind. But thank God, when we by faith came to the Lord Jesus, He not only forgave all our sins and unrighteousnesses, He also became our righteousness.

In other words, we can now stand before God as being righteous. Why so? Not, as we have just heard from Scripture, because we are righteous in ourselves nor because we have done something righteous. No, we have no righteousness: we can only stand before God today because we are clothed with Christ as our righteousness. This is all due to the fact that when God today looks upon us, He sees Christ; and because He sees Christ, He justifies us as being righteous. We now have a righteous standing before God all because He has made Christ to be our righteousness (I Corinthians 1:30).

Our Life in Christ and God's Life

It is true that because we are clothed with Christ as our righteousness, we have a standing or position before God. We can go and stand before Him because Christ is our righteousness. That is quite true. But Christ as our righteousness gives us more than a position or standing before God; He as our righteousness is also our life, for His life in us is righteous: the very nature of His life is righteous.

To say that a person manifests righteousness in his or her conduct is more than it being a matter of having done an act or deed that is deemed to be righteous. It is true, of course, that there are righteous acts, deeds, and conduct or behavior; nevertheless, in the Scriptures the notion of "righteousness" in one's conduct is considered to be more than doing one, two, or more acts which are righteous; it is also viewed as manifesting an aspect or feature of one's character, which stems from the nature of that person's being. And in referencing *God's* character the apostle John declared that He is righteous and that we Christians know it: "… ye know that he is righteous …" (I John 2:29a).

From this and other passages of Scripture we are given to understand that God not only *acts* righteously (indeed, He *always* acts that way), He himself *is righteous* according to the very nature of His divine life. Since God cannot deny himself, it becomes obvious that He cannot do anything *un*righteous. And why? Because for Him to do so would be contrary to the very character of His nature. Indeed, God's actions must conform to what He is by nature. To sum up, therefore, both God's *being* righteous and His *doing* righteously stem from, and define, God's nature and His character.

Our Practice

"Children, let no man lead you astray; he that practices righteousness is righteous, even as he [Christ] is righteous" (I John 3:7); "… every one who practices righteousness is begotten of him [God]" (I John 2:29b). Having been begotten of God and having thus received the divine life in Christ, that life is a righteous one in us. Accordingly, possessing this righteous life, we need to practice righteousness by doing acts righteously. For if we do sinful or unrighteous deeds, such conduct will be contrary to the nature of the new life in us. But if we live by the righteous life of Christ that is within us, then we shall be practicing righteousness.

Now as noted earlier, it is not sufficient for us to simply know and rest upon the fact that we have a position before God of *being* righteous because we have been clothed with Christ as our righteousness; on the contrary, we must also *live* righteously on this earth—we must practice righteousness. Yet, not in the sense of observing or keeping a law but in the sense of living out that law in a righteous manner. Otherwise, our conscience will not give us any peace because we are acting differently from what God is.

So, being righteous and doing righteously have their root or origin in a life—even the life of God in Christ. And if we follow this righteous life and allow it to be developed in us along the lines of various essential traits or features of character, we shall have those same aspects of the divine character as aspects of our character, too. Every believer should therefore be characterized by the righteousness of God. If He has delivered us from the sins of unrighteousness, then the first obligation in our Christian life is to conduct ourselves righteously.

We will recall that the Corinthian believers had been defrauding one another and fighting against each other; moreover, they had even gone so far as to go to court against each other. Paul therefore warned them in the following fashion:

> But ye do wrong, and defraud, and this your brethren. Do ye not know that unrighteous persons shall not inherit the kingdom of God? Do not err: neither fornicators, nor idolaters, nor adulterers, nor those who make women of themselves, nor who abuse themselves with men, nor thieves, nor covetous, nor drunkards, nor abusive persons, nor the rapacious, shall inherit the kingdom of God. And these things were some of you; but ye have been washed, but ye have been sanctified, but ye have been justified in the name of the Lord Jesus, and by the Spirit of our God (I Corinthians 6:8-11).

It was pointed out a few moments ago that the first, most basic obligation of the Christian is to behave righteously, for this is due to the fact that God has delivered the Christian from unrighteousness and granted him/her a righteous life, even the life of Christ. And hence, every Christian must live righteously by practicing righteousness.

Allow me to inquire: Do we followers of Christ have a sense of righteousness in ourselves? I am afraid that too many of us live quite loosely and carelessly, with the result that we compromise in many ways: an indication that we lack a strong sense of righteousness. If we do not have that strong sense, we cannot live righteously.

The Surpassing Righteousness

" … unless your righteousness surpass [or, excel in quality] that of the scribes and Pharisees, ye shall in no wise enter into the kingdom of the heavens" (Matthew 5:20). In Jesus' day the Pharisees and scribes in Israel had their own type or level of righteousness. What was the righteousness of these Israelite religious leaders? They kept the letter of the law, put on a good appearance, and seemed to do all that Jehovah God had required; but it was only a surface-level of righteousness. In other words, it was superficial, dead, and hypocritical in nature. Essentially, those Jewish religious leaders violated the *spirit* of the law altogether. Still, they had strictly observed what they considered to be their view of righteousness.

So the Lord declared that unless a person's righteousness excel in quality the righteousness of the scribes and the Pharisees of His day, no one could enter God's kingdom. Why so? Because the righteousness of Jesus' disciples must not be at the surface level but has to be deeper. As Christians our righteousness is not to be according to the letter of the law but must be according to the spirit of the law. Our righteousness is not to be hypocritical but is to be most real. Moreover, it is not dead but living.

With respect to this latter observation, namely, that our righteous acts should have a living, not a dead, quality to them, let us be reminded that the Bible has symbolically equated "the righteousnesses" (Darby) or "the righteous acts" (ASV) of the saints to bright (or, shining) and pure linen: "… it was given to her [the Lamb's bride, i.e., the glorious church] that she should be clothed in fine linen, bright and pure; for the fine linen is the righteousnesses of the saints" (Revelation 19:8). Not only are the righteous acts of the saints of God described here as being pure linen but also as being bright or glistening white linen. Which is to say that these righteous acts are not only pure in quality but also very much alive in quality.

Why this description? It is because these righteousnesses of the saints are the result of the Christ life within them which is righteous in nature. Were we believers to try performing so-called acts of righteousness in an outward self-motivating way, they would appear to be pale and death-like. In contrast to that outcome, if we adhere to and follow the righteous life of Christ within us, then acts which are truly righteous in nature shall begin to come forth, and whose quality or state is pure, bright, and full of life.

Jesus' so-called Sermon on the Mount teaches us righteousness (Matthew chs. 5-7): it instructs us regarding how Christians should live on earth as though they are living in the kingdom of the heavens. For as was observed earlier, Jesus had made it clear that unless a person's righteousness excels or surpasses in quality that of the scribes and Pharisees of His day in Israel, that one cannot even enter, let alone be in, the kingdom of the heavens. That, of course, was what the Lord Jesus had said early on in His so-called hillside sermon (5:20). And having declared that practical spiritual truth to His disciples, Jesus had immediately begun putting forth a series of examples to illustrate what He had in mind. And in each of them Jesus is found contrasting the righteous but lesser standard of the outward conformity to the Mosaic code with the surpassing righteous standard of God's heavenly kingdom. What therefore follows is but the first of the Lord's five examples.

> Ye have heard that it was said to the ancients, Thou shalt not [murder]; but whosoever shall [murder] shall be [guilty before the court]. But I say unto you, that every one that is lightly angry [or, angry without cause] with his brother shall be [guilty before the court]; [and] whosoever shall say to his brother, Raca [Aramaic for:

empty-head or good for nothing], shall be [guilty before the supreme court—i.e., the Sanhedrin]; [and] whoever shall say, [You] Fool, shall be [guilty enough to go into] the hell of fire. If therefore thou shouldest offer thy gift at the altar, and there shouldest remember that thy brother has something against thee, leave there thy gift before the altar, and first go, be reconciled to thy brother, and then come and offer thy gift (5:21-24 Darby, with bracketed words NASB mgn).

Here we discern that the righteousness of the scribes and Pharisees was only the outward *letter* of the Mosaic Law: Thou shalt not murder; and as long as a person does not murder someone, that person has exhibited righteousness. Nevertheless, oh how these Jewish religious leaders *hated* people and held them in contempt! They naturally dared not commit the act of murder because the Law forbade it; even so, in their hearts they were full of *anger* and hatred. Yet the Lord had taught here that we His disciples should not even be "lightly" angry with our brethren. For though there may be cause for legitimate righteous anger towards someone on occasion, Scripture elsewhere teaches that if that be the case, we nonetheless must not sin nor let the sun go down upon our wrath (Ephesians 4:26, quoting Psalm 4:4a).

Throughout Jesus' hillside sermonic teaching as recorded in these three chapters of Matthew we find that the Lord is instructing His own people to live righteously in this world. That we are not only not to commit sin (an outward act) but also to live righteously from the heart (an inward reality) both in the sight of God and with and before man.

Moreover, in what can perhaps be termed a sub-summary statement within Jesus' overall teaching on the hillside, He instructed His disciples to "seek … first the kingdom of God and his righteousness, and all these things shall be added unto you" (6:33). What are "these things" to which the Lord made reference? And how should His followers live on the earth in relation to "all these things"? Do we not live our lives on earth quite occupied with the things of this earth: what we shall eat? what we shall drink? and with what we shall be clothed? However, Jesus teaches us God's priority for our lives: "Seek ye first the kingdom of God and his righteousness ..." It is kingdom righteousness which is required of God's people first and foremost in their lives, and if that is adhered to, then all these things with which we are preoccupied shall be provided to us.

Some people, though, assert that they can never ever keep Jesus' hillside sermon. That is in fact quite true: no one can do so in and of themselves. It is only by the life of Christ in us Christians that any of us can live righteously as described in great detail in these three chapters of the Bible. But, you may ask, Is the nature of that Christ-life marked by such surpassing righteousness? Yes, indeed! Yet, that being so, then why, it may be asked, is this not being practiced in so many of our lives today? Why, further, does such righteousness not become a character-trait in us? I believe it is because too many of us rebel, fight and struggle against God. We simply do not yield ourselves to His will and cooperate with the Spirit of God.

Dear brethren, this is to be the first and foremost operating principle in our Christian lives. If we Christians cannot live righteously, how can we live spiritually? I am afraid that at times we are inclined to divorce these two conditions—as though to be spiritual is to be above being righteous. Indeed, we may tend to think that we can do many godly things if we are spiritual. Not so. That is nothing but pseudo-spirituality. If we do not live righteously on earth, we are not spiritual at all. Simply put, to be spiritual is to be righteous in our living on the earth. This righteousness is one of the most important aspects of the Christ-character, and which has to be developed, nurtured, and matured in each one of us.

The Personal Cost in Our Being Righteous

Having said that, it is necessary for me to have us understand that for a trait of Christ's character to be developed in us we shall have to pay some cost personally. For let us carefully note what the Lord Jesus had observed about this very matter at the outset of His hillside teaching of His disciples. In fact, it was the concluding beatitude of eight statements of blessing:

> Blessed they who are persecuted on account of righteousness, for *theirs* is the kingdom of the heavens. Blessed are ye when they may reproach and persecute you, and say every wicked thing against you, lying, for my sake. Rejoice and exult, for your reward is great in the heavens; for thus have they persecuted the prophets who were before you (Matthew 5:10-12).

Let us be clear that the development in us of an attribute of the Lord's character such as righteousness does not come about easily. In your wanting to be righteous it may at first be very hard for you: you may, in fact, suffer for it. Nevertheless, the Lord Jesus declared that those who are persecuted for the sake of righteousness are blessed.

Even so, for you to be righteous will not make you popular. Not only will you not have an easy life on account of being righteous, it will also not make you popular in the least because the whole unbelieving world is *un*righteous. For when the people of the world notice that you do not follow them, they will hate you, even as Jesus has prophesied. Realize this, however, that if you are persecuted for the sake of righteousness, rejoice—"for your reward is great in the heavens."

The Secret for Living Righteously

A Pure Conscience

How can we live righteously? And why is it that too often we do not live righteously? Moreover, what is the secret for living righteously? Perhaps a little explanation scripturally concerning mankind's conscience can be helpful here before attempting to address these questions.

When we were saved God quickened or made alive our dead spirit (Ephesians 2:5). In addition, because we had a wicked conscience He found it necessary to purify it from the heart (Hebrews 10:22b), inasmuch as our conscience had been seared or branded by our continual sinning (cf. I Timothy 4:2b ASV mgn). And therefore, even though our seared conscience still sensed something bothering it, nonetheless, the conscience did not feel or sense very much that something was amiss ethically or morally in our living. Now, however, God has purified our wicked conscience and given us a new one—a conscience which is clean, clear, open, soft, and highly sensitive.

What, then, is the work or use of the human conscience? It is that in us which tells us what is right and what is wrong in the sight of God. It is very important for a Christian to live by his or her conscience. Before we were saved we could not live by our conscience because it was for the most part dead and hence undependable, it having no standard. But when the Holy Spirit pricked our conscience (cf. Acts 2:37), it was awakened somewhat and began to discern somewhat between what is right and what is wrong before God. People of the world may declare: "I live by my conscience, I am therefore good"; but should the Holy Spirit prick those persons' conscience, then they shall truly begin to know their real situation and condition.

Once we become Christians we are to live righteously. Yet not by being told all the time how we should live nor by our posting rules for living on the walls of our homes. No, we are to live righteously by heeding the voice of our purified conscience which God gave us when we were saved. Indeed, this renewed conscience of ours now has God as its standard, and in and through our conscience God is speaking to us: He is telling us what is right and what is wrong. And hence, the apostle Paul could humbly and honestly assert: "I have lived before God in all good conscience until this day" and "I … exercise myself to have a conscience void of offence toward God and men always" (Acts 23:1b, 24:16, both vv. ASV).

The reason many Christians do not live righteously is because they are not attentive to the voice of their conscience. In our prior unregenerate state we all had bad habits and had done all kinds of things which we should not have done. And even after we were saved we may have still desired to do some of those same things. As a matter of fact, we may not even have realized at first that those things were considered wrong in God's sight. Later, though, whenever we might do such things we realize for sure that they are not right in His sight. Our conscience tells us this now. However, if we push our conscience aside by neglecting, ignoring, or reasoning against it, the result will be that the voice of conscience shall eventually grow silent, totally unheard. That is why Christians must learn to live by their conscience. And that is the secret for living righteously. It is by one's conscience being without offense that the Christian can live righteously before God and before men.

A Conscience Careful about Little Things

There is another reason why many Christians fail to live righteously. They incorrectly assume that the spiritual life is marked by having to deal with big things, big issues, big matters. Actually, however, the life with God consists mostly of having to deal with the small things of the day. Such wrong thinking on the part of these Christians will mean that they approach the handling of various small matters, which surely do come before them, in a careless manner, they musing within themselves by saying dismissively: "Oh, these little items of concern amount to nothing. Why should anyone be bothered listening to their conscience about such trivia? And besides, other Christians I know are treating the matter in the same way as I intend doing every time such trivia come before me."

Permit me to observe, however, that if Christians are very careless with respect to the small matters of everyday life, the result will be that they shall likewise be careless in their treatment of the big things. Yet, to live righteously before God, we need to be careful in all matters: not only the large ones but also the more frequent small ones. And this will require us to walk before God with a good conscience and to have continual dealings with our conscience. Even so, I must acknowledge from my own experience that at the beginning it is not that easy to do.

At this point in our discussion on this issue, allow me to put before you some practical examples of what I have in mind. Have you ever gone through your shelves and discovered that there were some books which you had borrowed but had never returned? Have you ever searched your home to see if there was anything that you might have acquired unrighteously? Is there anything which does not belong to you but you took it as your own? Does it ever bother you that though the church meeting begins at 10:30 you often arrive at 11:00? If your response to all these inquiries is "Yes," then one or more of their content could be construed as having been unrighteous conduct; which indicates that your conscience apparently did not bother you. Which also indicates that in treating these small matters carelessly, you were developing, not a righteous character-trait, but an unrighteous one.

The above exercise reveals how we Christians can be careless in those frequent daily small things which come before us; and hence, we have not lived righteously before God and man. Indeed, our careless conduct could even be deemed to be worse than that of the people of the world.

Let us consider further the following scenario. If we are going to meet someone of importance and we have an appointment with that person, we would never dare be late, would we? Yet, having appointments with God, we are often late, and perhaps we do not even show up; and furthermore, we may not even think about it at all. Such unrighteous behavior reflects the fact that we have not habituated ourselves to listening to the voice of our conscience.

Dear brethren, let us be reminded afresh that this character-trait of righteousness constitutes the very first pillar upon which the house of God is to be built. And to that end He wants to establish within each one of us the Christ-life character-trait of righteousness. Let us likewise take note of *this* truth as well, that the Lord Jesus not only is righteous in His character, He also is called—appropriately so in Scripture—The Righteous One (cf. I

John 2:1b). If righteousness is truly one aspect of our Lord's character, and it most certainly is, then we His followers must live righteously before God—and man, too—just as He had done while He was on this earth.

Overly Righteous

"Be not righteous overmuch; neither make thyself overwise: why shouldest thou destroy thyself?" (Ecclesiastes 7:16) This is a very strange verse in the Bible. We should definitely be righteous, but can we be overly righteous? Probably when we are under the light of God we would probably say to ourselves, "Well, we are not righteous, we instead are underly righteous." Yet here Solomon advises us to "not be overly righteous or overly wise. Why should you destroy your life?"

What does Solomon's advice mean? I feel that what is meant here is this: Not that we can really be overly righteous but that we are always underly so. However, when we try to be righteous by our own effort in the manner in which the Pharisees and the scribes did, we in reality are developing a degree of self-righteousness. Our sense of self-righteousness may become so great that we think everybody else is wrong; which is to say, that we think we are the only ones who are righteous. We begin to look down upon everybody around us and begin to criticize them. And the result is that we are destroying our spiritual lives by our being righteous overmuch, which in reality is not righteousness at all.

There could be the frequent danger that as we are attempting to live righteously we may unintentionally veer off from the correct path and become self-righteous. That, I believe, is what is meant here by Solomon's warning: Be not overly righteous lest you come to think of yourself as being most righteous in God's sight. With the consequence being, however, that you become hard, harsh, and critical, and end up setting yourself up as a judge of everybody else. Yet Jesus said, "Judge not, that ye may not be judged" (Matthew 7:1).

By way of conclusion, it is my belief that the Lord is building God's house, which is the church. And as He is about the business of building God's house, He is wanting to develop His character in us; for it is Christ's sevenfold traits of character in us His people that are to be the strong pillars which shall support God's House of Rest and Peace. May we truly humble ourselves before God and be very practical. May we be willing to be dealt with by the Holy Spirit along the lines of very practical issues in our lives so that He may develop and mature in us a real sense of righteousness which shall serve as one of the seven essential pillars in support of God's house. That, I firmly believe, is what He wants to accomplish.

Our heavenly Father, we do acknowledge that we are underly righteous. We are far below what Thou art. Father, we put ourselves in Thy hands and ask that Thy Holy Spirit develop Christ's character in us and manifest His righteousness out from our lives. We want to be righteous, because Thou art righteous. In the name of our Lord Jesus. Amen.

Pillar 2—The Character-Trait of Diligence

Proverbs 10:4—He cometh to want that dealeth with a slack hand; but the hand of the diligent maketh rich.

Proverbs 12:24—The hand of the diligent shall bear rule; but the slothful hand shall be under tribute.

Proverbs 12:27—A slothful man will not catch his prey, but the diligent man will get precious wealth (RSV).

Proverbs 13:4—A sluggard's soul desireth and hath nothing; but the soul of the diligent shall be made fat.

Proverbs 15:19—The way of the sluggard is as a hedge of thorns; but the path of the upright is made plain.

Proverbs 19:15—Slothfulness casteth into a deep sleep, and the idle soul shall suffer hunger.

Proverbs 19:24—A sluggard burieth his hand in the dish, and will not even bring it to his mouth again.

Proverbs 20:4—The sluggard will not plough by reason of the winter; he shall beg in harvest, and have nothing.

Proverbs 21:25—The desire of the sluggard killeth him; for his hands refuse to work.

Proverbs 22:13—The sluggard saith, There is a lion without, I shall be killed in the streets!

Proverbs 22:29—Hast thou seen a man diligent in his work? He shall stand before kings; he shall not stand before the mean [or, before obscure men NASB].

Proverbs 24:30-34—I went by the field of a sluggard, and by the vineyard of a man void of understanding; and lo, it was all grown over with thistles, and nettles had covered the face thereof, and its stone wall was broken down. Then I looked, I took it to heart; I saw, I received instruction: —A little sleep, a little slumber, a little folding of the hands to rest! So shall thy poverty come as a roving plunderer, and thy penury as an armed man.

The character-trait which the second pillar symbolically represents and which is present in the proverbs of Solomon is that of diligence. Indeed, the various verses set forth above clearly demonstrate the fact that throughout these sayings of King Solomon there are numerous times when not only the *word* diligent but also the *thought* of diligence is everywhere present among these proverbs.

Our God is a very diligent deity. His Son declared this while on earth: "My Father worketh until now, and I work" also (John 5:17 ASV). Diligence is an attribute of God's character. And since our Father-God is diligent, He requires of us His sons and daughters to develop the same character-trait in ourselves: that of diligence.

Concerning God's Son, the Son of man the Lord Jesus, we find in the Gospel of Mark one very revealing word descriptive of this same character-feature of diligence. And in the Authorized and the American Standard Versions of the Bible this descriptive term appears in the Gospel no less than nineteen times. Now that descriptive term is the word straightway—or translated as immediately in other Bible versions. With respect to the Lord Jesus in His ministry on earth, His work was always immediately to be accomplished, He never putting off till *later* what He realized should be done *now*. In fact, this latter habit among Spanish-speaking people is best summed up in their oft-repeated use of the word in Spanish for tomorrow, *mañana*, signifying the putting off to "an indefinite time in the future" (Webster's) the accomplishing of that which should have been done *today*. Actually, in all of human nature—and not just in the Spanish-speaking peoples of the world—there is the tendency towards slothfulness, laziness seemingly being deeply embedded in mankind's very bones.

Our Fallen Nature: Slothfulness

God's Original Design

When God first created man He had provided everything for him in the Garden of Eden. He had planted many beautiful trees, all of which were "good for food." Even so, God did not put man in the Garden simply to live a life of leisure; rather, He commanded man to till and guard the Garden; thus indicating that God had not wanted man to be lazy there.

Though it is quite true that God had provided everything necessary for food and shelter, it was never His intent for man to merely maintain a living. Yes, if man wished to live just for himself in the Edenic garden, he could simply pluck the fruit off its many fruit trees for his food and live out his life continually in that manner. But no, God indicated to man that he had not been placed in the Garden merely to maintain a living; "beyond that," instructed God to man, "you are in the Garden to till and to guard it for My glory" (see Genesis 2:9a, 15).

Now before sin had entered the picture there were no thorns, thistles or weeds present in the Edenic garden; nevertheless, God told man to till the Garden. Why so? Well, most likely the soil around the base of the trees needed to be loosened up so that they could bear more fruit to the glory of God. Moreover, these trees surely needed to be pruned now and then so that the same result could be achieved.

Furthermore, the first human couple—Adam and Eve— were told by God not only to till the Garden but to guard its environs as well. Why was this necessary? Well, since the Garden lacked any wall, this meant that these two would be needed to be the Garden's watchmen who would have to be on watch all the time against the intrusion of the enemy of both themselves and God. And if they were to be the Garden's policemen who, as it were, would have to be "on the beat" day in and day out, these two could not in the least live a lazy life. To the contrary, their lives would be marked by being busily occupied for the glory of God.

The Fall of Man

One day, however, for some reason Eve was alone. She was not on duty with her husband assisting in tilling and guarding. Instead, she had apparently wandered away from Adam and her shared duty and was now engaged in daydreaming as she gazed at one particular Garden tree. "Ahh," she said to herself, "this tree looks so beautiful and its fruit looks quite good to eat." Yet God had said that of the fruit of all the Garden's trees these two could eat except the fruit of the tree of the knowledge of good and evil; for in the day that they should eat its fruit, they would die. "But why so?" she thought to herself while standing and daydreaming in front of this tree. But it was at this moment that the enemy, Satan, appeared on the scene in the form of a serpent and proceeded to tempt her to sin. And so, Eve (and subsequently Adam also) ate of this tree's fruit and both consequently fell into the sin of disobedience (Genesis 2:8-9, 15-17; 3:1-7).

Is there not a very important lesson in this for us all to learn? It is not good for people to be at leisure all of the time nor good to be lazy. For oftentimes it is while we are at leisure or unoccupied with work or perhaps daydreaming that temptations come and, like Eve, we can fall into the snare of the devil.

The Merciful Punishment

After the Fall of man God disciplined both the man and his wife. To Adam He said that henceforth he would have to labor in sorrowful toil upon the ground of the earth; in order for Adam to earn his bread and make a living for himself he would need to labor by the sweat of his face in the midst of thistles, thorns and weeds (Genesis 3:17-19a). On the one hand God's pronouncement was punishment; on the other hand it was disguised mercy. And why? God realized that if man did not labor or be required to work to earn a living, he would engage in other pursuits which might lead to sin. Hence, by God keeping man away from idleness it could keep him from committing many sins.

It was the same with Eve, who was told by God that she (and by inference all women after her) would experience travail in giving birth to children (3:16a). In one sense God's pronouncement meant punishment, but it was accompanied by mercy in that, by having to be busily occupied with children, she would more likely live a godly life than otherwise.

Let us all realize that God does not desire any person to be lazy and loafing about, for such a lifestyle is not good for man. Yet, it must be acknowledged that following the Fall, fallen man's nature developed into laziness, the latter having become deeply embedded in our very bones. For if there is an opportunity for a person to do so, he or she will surely follow the path of least resistance. Just as water flows easily downward rather than by the far more difficult and obviously impossible upward direction, we fallen human beings will more often than not choose to tread the easier path. In fact, we will always prefer the life of ease and leisure and think to ourselves, "Now, that is the real life!" God, however, looks at this matter quite differently: He wishes to reestablish in us fallen human beings the character-trait of diligence.

What Diligence Is

What is diligence? The very word means "the applying of oneself" or, as Webster's dictionary defines the term, diligence is a "devoted and painstaking application to accomplish an undertaking." Furthermore, in view of this definition, since a diligent person will be applying himself/herself with devotion, zeal and earnestness to accomplishing a given task, it most likely will involve some pain as well, but the person proceeds to do the task anyway. By which is meant that the task in one way or another may be difficult, troublesome, unpleasant, even irksome or annoying; yet the person perseveres anyway in applying himself/herself in a devoted and painstaking manner to accomplish the task. Altogether, then, that is the meaning of the word diligence.

Now there is a difference between being busy and being diligent. You may be very busy but you may not necessarily be diligent in your busyness. Why so? Because diligence is an attribute or a trait of a person's character, and hence, it is not the act or deed associated with being busy. For instance, you may be put into a situation wherein you are kept busy by force because your boss is standing nearby and is commanding: "Do that task quickly; quickly, quickly!" Thus, you are busily occupied but you are not manifesting diligence in your busyness at all. Moreover, in this and other situations, if you have been busy doing a given task for a while, there may come a moment in which you feel you deserve to have a break, and so you rest. Such is obviously not the meaning of diligence.

Diligence is a feature of one's character. If you possess this character-trait, it will mean that no matter what you may be doing, you will be applying yourself with zeal, eagerness and earnestness despite any pain, difficulty or unpleasantness involved in so doing. Diligence is therefore not a matter of what the task is with which you may be occupied; nor is it a matter of how long you may be busy in performing the said task; but it *is* a matter of the very *way* or *manner* with which you take upon yourself the accomplishing of the task. Now *that* is diligence.

How Diligence Can Be Established in Us

The issue before us, then, is this: How can we be diligent? Since, as was indicated earlier, laziness is an aspect of our fallen character, and also since in and of ourselves we are unable to change that reality, how *can* we be diligent? Thank God, the answer is to be found in the fact that He has put a new life in us—even that of His Son Jesus—and whose one particular character-trait, among others, is the attribute of diligence. And just as Jesus was diligent throughout His entire walk on the earth, even so, His life in us, if allowed to grow and be lived out, will lead to the establishment of that same character-trait of diligence in us as well.

Confessing Our Laziness

Practically speaking, we first of all need to come before God and pray: "Oh God, I must confess that in me there is no diligence—I admit that I am lazy." Unless we are brought to that point there is not much hope for Him to reestablish the attribute of diligence in our character. Initially, therefore, we will need to allow the Holy Spirit to convict us of our slothfulness and be willing to confess the same before God. We need to admit that we often push matters aside which ought to be done today by saying to ourselves that we will do them tomorrow; yet, when tomorrow arrives, we repeat the same intention: "Tomorrow."

Hence, we must acknowledge before God that our past behavior has been of thinking that if we can get by without accomplishing certain duties today, we end up attempting to salve our conscience by saying to ourselves, *"Mañana, mañana."* And this, we need to confess, has unfortunately become nearly a habit in us.

Allow me to inquire: Has the Holy Spirit begun to touch that fallen character of yours? Has the Spirit of God spoken to you concerning your slothfulness? Has He ever touched your conscience when you pushed an undertaking aside that should have been done that day? Have you felt uneasy about the matter before God? Have you ever been brought before God? Have you ever been brought to that place? Have you ever *tried* to be diligent? Now if such matters have been true of you, then one day you will arrive at the point of saying, "Lord, there is no diligence in me. If You want me to be diligent, *You* will have to do it, for there is nothing in me which can make this possible. I acknowledge that I am a lazy person." One may lose face in acknowledging that, but before God we have to be honest.

Diligence is not a trait of our fallen character. Ours is just the opposite: it is a trait of laziness. When we finally realize that laziness is a sin before God, and that we in ourselves cannot overcome it, we will cast ourselves upon Him and learn to depend upon *His* life. And when that happens, that will be the beginning of the development in us of this character-trait of diligence.

Cooperating with the Holy Spirit

After you have confessed that there is not that character-trait of diligence in you, and after you have ceased trying to improve yourself since it is beyond improving (otherwise, if it could be improved, then our "old man" needed not to have been crucified with Christ on the cross; Romans 6:6a), then you will need to learn in your daily life to be open to the Spirit of God in showing you in what way you are not diligent.

We have to be humble enough before God to allow Him by His Spirit to show us wherein we are not diligent. And as the Holy Spirit begins to convict us of this lack, let us learn to cast ourselves upon God's mercy and upon His life, praying: "Lord, I want to be diligent. May the Lord Jesus be my diligence." Let us cooperate with the Holy Spirit, yield ourselves to the Lord Jesus, and let His life take over and live through us.

Denying Ourselves and Taking Up Our Cross

In the course of that process, it will surely involve, as was briefly alluded to earlier, the intruding into our daily life of various, often unexpected, demands upon our time and attention which can frequently trigger all kinds of mental, psychological, and perhaps even physical discomfort and pain, and which requires some degree of discipline on our part in diligently addressing those intrusions that are legitimate. And for the most part these are small matters, they coming to us in the form of untimely interruptions, or tasks demanded of us which may strike us as irksome, annoying, troublesome, even upsetting in nature. And yet, our responsibility as *diligent* followers of Christ is to undertake the accomplishing of these matters faithfully, completely, and—when called for—in a timely manner. All this is but one of the reasons why the Lord Jesus felt it necessary to instruct His disciples as follows: "If anyone would come after

Me, he must deny himself, take up his cross *daily*, and follow Me" (see Luke 9:23).

For us simply to be willing for the life of Christ to live in and out from us is not sufficient. Sometimes we pray, "Lord, I am willing to let You live in me"; but that is not enough. There is a crucifying process involved. By the grace of God we must learn to deny ourselves, take up our particular cross, and follow the Lord Jesus. If we adhere to this process—which involves both pain and discipline—Christ's life shall begin to flow.

Allow me to use a little personal example of mine here to illustrate what I have in mind with regard to this necessary process of pain and discipline involving the cross. This personal example revolves around the task of writing letters. Suppose someone has written a letter to me in which there are certain important matters needing a response from me. Suppose, further, that there is a time limit requiring an answer from me by a certain date. I do not know about you brethren but I know what often happens with me in a situation like this: I generally will put the letter aside and tell myself, "I'll answer it by and by but I'm not in the mood to do so right now. When the mood strikes me, then I'll answer the letter." However, what ends up happening is that my incoming letters commence piling up until eventually one day I will sit myself down and write letter after letter after letter.

There are times as well that I forget to give reply to an important letter needing to be answered here and another important letter needing a reply there. I simply put them aside. For instance, last week someone called me long distance asking me about certain matters he had written in a letter to me that I had completely forgotten about answering. His letter was there on my desk, and I had meant to answer it; but not being in the mood, it had completely slipped my mind. This behavior of mine wearies people, forcing them to have to call me even long distance,[*] which causes me to feel ashamed over the matter.

This that I have shared is merely one single example among many such tasks which should be done by us; nevertheless, we shall find that there is a delaying tactic or other kinds of tactics in our old fallen nature which prevent our being diligent followers of Christ. Consequently, there are times when we need to place ourselves under the Spirit's discipline. Though we may not feel like applying ourselves in accomplishing various needful tasks which intrude themselves into our daily life, we nonetheless must, by the grace of God, look to the Lord to be our diligence in this or that matter. It may be somewhat painful to our souls because the task before us may be distasteful, troublesome, or not in the least to our liking. Even so, that is precisely how the diligent attribute in the character of Christ's life can be established and grow in us, and then flow out from us.

The Thoughts, Attitudes and Feelings of the Sluggard

What are the thoughts, attitudes, and feelings of the slothful person or the sluggard? Well, according to just those verses from the book of Proverbs which were quoted at the outset of this message, we learn—in no particular order—the following insights into the life of the sluggard. To begin with, the sluggard's soul has a desire, but that being all he does, he gains or obtains nothing. And why? Because he will not do anything; he refuses to work. Moreover, the sluggard's desire, which leads to nothing, ultimately kills him spiritually; that is to say, his soul continually feels unsatisfied and therefore discontented (13:4, 21:25).

The attitude of the sluggard is, that it is *always* winter; and since one cannot plough and sow in the wintertime, therefore, when harvest season comes around, this slothful one has nothing

---

[*] The reader should bear in mind that long-distance phone calls back in the 1960s were expensive compared to the cost of a local phone call; whereas the current long-distance cost may be the same as a local call and/or included with a given phone plan.—*The Publishers*

60

to show for his/her attitude (20:4). In contrast to the attitude of the sluggard, the diligent Jesus once observed: "You disciples of Mine, you say that there are yet four months before harvesttime; but I tell you to look upon the fields all about you: the grain therein is already white ready for harvest" (see John 4:35).

What, I ask again, are the attitudes and feelings like in the slothful, lazy person? He cries out: "There is a lion outside! I shall be killed out on the streets!" Hence, he says he cannot go outside (22:13). Oh, the sluggard is continually waiting for a better time, an easier, more convenient environment. Yet he fails to realize that the problem resides with him.

What will happen to the slothful person? According to these proverbs of Solomon, the sluggard will constantly be in want. Not having done anything, he shall constantly be hungry and poverty-stricken (10:4, 19:15). In fact, the sluggard will have grown so slothful that though burying his hand in the food dish, he has become too lazy to even bring the food up to his mouth (19:24)! Now because the slothful person is always seeking to enjoy having a bit more rest and a little more sleep, the consequence is that poverty and want easily come to his door (20:34). Finally, his end is that he can never rule but will himself be ruled by being forcefully consigned to slave labor (12:24).

Oh, how all of us need to be disciplined by God's Spirit in order that this slothfulness of ours may be dealt with. May the character-trait of diligence be established in each one of us.

Areas about Which to Be Diligent

Keeping and Guarding Our Hearts

"Watch over your heart with all diligence, for from it flow the springs of life" (Proverbs 4:23 NASB). We must be diligent in watching over, guarding and keeping our heart, for it is the center of our being. Not only is the heart the center of our physical being; we are told here in Scripture that it also—in a spiritual, moral sense—is the center of our spiritual life. Since from our heart flow the springs of life, the Bible says that we need to be most diligent in guarding our heart lest it be enticed, cheated, deceived, or even hardened.

How, then, can we diligently keep our heart? The only way is to give our heart to the Lord and let Him watch over and keep it (23:26a). That same proverb goes on to say that by giving our hearts to the Lord, our eyes will observe and delight in His ways (v. 26b). Truly, we do not know how to guard and keep our hearts. And why? Because they are so deceitful that they can even deceive *ourselves* (Jeremiah 17:9). Hence, the only way to diligently keep our hearts is for us to give them over to the Lord. We therefore need to pray: "Lord, my heart is Yours. Guard it so that I may love You with all my heart. Do keep my heart from all deception. And if there be any deception therein, then show that to me. Indeed, Lord, search and examine my heart and see if there be any wicked, hurtful or grievous way in it, even as You have said in Your word of Scripture; and lead me in the everlasting way" (see Psalm 139:23-24).

Moreover, if we truly give our hearts to the Lord, He will watch over and guard them. How will He do this? Another Scripture informs us as follows: "Today, if you hear His voice, you will not harden your heart" (see Psalm 95:7c-8a). We will hear the Lord's voice by His Spirit if we have truly given our hearts to Him: the Holy Spirit will speak to us, and whenever there may be any problem, difficulty, or tendency to waywardness, the Spirit of the Lord will speak to us and we shall hear His voice and respond accordingly.

On the one hand, the Lord by His Spirit guards and keeps our hearts if we give them over to Him; on the other hand, we, too, must guard our hearts above all things else, since it is the treasure of our life. If something turns wrong with our hearts, then our entire spiritual life will collapse. And hence, this is where we need to apply ourselves with all diligence: we must be vigilant in keeping our hearts, and thus we cannot afford to be lazy or slothful or careless in this vital matter. Diligence must ever and always be exercised.

Seeking God

"But without faith it is impossible to please him. For he that draws near to God must believe that he is, and that he is a rewarder of them who seek him out [or, "them that diligently seek him" KJV] (Hebrews 11:6). "Seek him out" means to "diligently seek him." We need to seek God with *diligence*. Why so? Because sometimes when you seek Him, He seems to evade you; and if you give up, you will not find Him. You therefore have to continue to seek Him diligently, and then He will reward you. Allow me to inquire: In seeking God do we rise up early in the morning, and do we study His word with diligence? Seek Him diligently and He will reward you. You will find Him if you do.

Keeping God's Commandments

"Ye shall diligently keep the commandments of Jehovah your God, and His testimonies, and His statutes, which He hath commanded thee" (Deuteronomy 6:17). We should diligently keep His commandments. When the Lord speaks to us, how do we respond? Do we say "yes" but wait a while before obeying? Or is our response like that when God instructed Abraham to offer up his only son of promise—Isaac? Do we recall what He did? Early the next morning he rose up and went forward immediately and obeyed. Let us also be diligent, like Abraham, in keeping God's commandments.

Building Characteristics

But for this very reason also, using therewith all diligence, in your faith have also virtue, in virtue knowledge, in knowledge temperance, in temperance endurance, in endurance godliness, in godliness brotherly love, in brotherly love love: for these things existing and abounding in you make you to be neither idle nor unfruitful as regards the knowledge of our Lord Jesus Christ; for he with whom these things are not present is blind, short-sighted, and has forgotten the purging of his former sins. Wherefore the rather, brethren, use diligence to make your calling and election sure, for doing these things ye will never fall; For thus shall the entrance into the everlasting kingdom of our Lord and Saviour Jesus Christ be richly furnished unto you (II Peter 1:5-11).

In the development in us of Christ's various attributes of character (which is what this passage is concerned with), we must be diligent. If we are not, then the character of Christ cannot be produced in us. We have to apply ourselves and cooperate daily with the Holy Spirit in order to have the divine character in all its features established and matured in us.

Keeping the Unity of the Spirit

"… using diligence to keep the unity of the Spirit in the uniting bond of peace. There is one body and one Spirit, as ye have been also called in one hope of your calling; one Lord, one faith, one baptism; one God and Father of all, who is over all, and through all, and in us all" (Ephesians 4:3-6). We must diligently keep the unity of the Spirit in the uniting bond of peace. We who are God's people need to maintain the unity of the Spirit. And how? By applying ourselves diligently in this matter. How easy it is for God's people to be divided! How easy it is for God's people to be at odds with one another! How we therefore need to use diligence to keep the unity of the Spirit in the sevenfold oneness in God. This is a vital spiritual area in which we have to be diligent. If we are not, we will not possess it. Instead, we shall lose this unity.

Serving the Lord

"Strive diligently to present thyself approved to God, a workman that has not to be ashamed, cutting in a straight line the word of truth" (II Timothy 2:15). " … or he that exhorts, in exhortation; he that gives, in simplicity; he that leads, with diligence; he that shews mercy, with cheerfulness … [and] as to diligent zealousness, not slothful; in spirit, fervent; serving the Lord" (Romans 12:8, 11). We must be diligent in serving the Lord. In our serving Him we need to be diligent. We should be like the good servants, and not like the wicked one who was slothful (Matthew 25:14-30, noting especially v.26a).

Spreading the Good News

"Be urgent in season and out of season, convict, rebuke, encourage, with all longsuffering and doctrine" (II Timothy 4:2). "Walk in wisdom towards those without, redeeming opportunities" [or, "seizing opportunities"—per Darby's note for Ephesians 5:16] (Colossians 4:5). These verses are actually expressive of the desire of the apostle Paul for his readers to be diligent in spreading the good news of the gospel in terms of both evangelism towards the unbelievers ("those without") and the instruction of the saints. And for success to be achieved in both, diligence is required.

The Blessings and Rewards of Diligence

If we are diligent, what will be the result? According to the proverbs of Solomon, the diligent person will obtain precious wealth (12:29, cf. 10:4). The man diligent in his work shall not stand among obscure men but he shall stand among kings (22:29). In fact, the diligent person shall rule (12:24) and shall reign with Christ in His millennial kingdom (Revelation 20:6b). The one with diligent hands will not be in want but shall make himself rich (10:4) so that he may have more to give. Furthermore, if we are diligent, we shall be able to serve instead of being served (cf. Mark 10:45), and thus be used by the Lord.

These, then, are the many blessings and rewards for those who are diligent and not slothful or idle. May God establish in each one of us Christ's character-trait of diligence, and thus bring glory to God.

**Lord, we do acknowledge that in ourselves there is
not this trait of diligence. We do confess how easy it is**

for us to follow the easy path—to be slothful. We acknowledge that we do not even have the strength to be diligent. But Lord, Thou art our life and Thou art our strength. And, so, we commit ourselves to Thee, asking Thee to develop this character-trait of diligence in every one of us. May Thy Holy Spirit watch over us, convict us, and bring us into this daily practice of diligence. Oh, we ask Thee that day by day we may learn it in small things, so that this character-aspect of Thine may be established in us; and that Thou mayest build Thy church with such a quality of character—all to the praise of Thy glory. We thank Thee, Lord. In Thy precious name. Amen.

Pillar 3—The Character-Trait of Love

Proverbs 14:30—A sound heart is the life of the flesh; but envy the rottenness of the bones.

Proverbs 15:17—Better is a meal of herbs where love is, than a fatted ox and hatred therewith.

Proverbs 17:9—He that covereth transgression seeketh love; but he that bringeth a matter up again separateth very friends.

Proverbs 17:17—The friend loveth at all times, and a brother is born for adversity.

Proverbs 22:11—He that loveth pureness of heart, upon whose lips is grace, the king is his friend.

Among the seven pillars that Wisdom Personified—even Christ—is erecting, in support of the House of Rest and Peace which He is building for His Father-God, is the Pillar of Love. Now we oftentimes view love as simply an emotion. It *is* that, no question about it; but love is that which is much deeper than merely an emotion. For let us consider what the Bible has in part asserted about love, which is, that "God is love" (I John 4:16b). Love is therefore one of many aspects, traits, or characteristics of the divine nature of God. And with regard to ourselves, as this love of His is expressed and practiced by and through us His sons and daughters, there is gradually developed and ultimately established in us this character-trait of love that is an essential part of the divine nature (cf. II Peter 1:4b).

God's Love: More Than an Emotion

Our God is the God of love. With Him, His loving is not simply an emotional reaction to something or someone outside himself. His love runs deeper than emotion, whereas with man, to love is chiefly a reaction to the circumstance, environment, or individual with what or with whom the person has contact. If, for example, you are stimulated to react to someone in a positive, pleasant way, you will perhaps be reacting with an emotional expression called love. But if you are stimulated to react to someone in a negative, unpleasant way, you will most likely be reacting with an emotional expression called hate.

Furthermore, if love is simply an emotion, then it is transient in nature and therefore subject to change. That love is being governed by the outward circumstance, environment, or a particular other person. Such love is never going to be steady. But the love which is a character-trait of God's divine nature is permanent and thus never changes. Outside environment or the kind of person an individual is does not determine how God's love will react or be expressed. He just loves regardless because He is who He is: God is love.

First of all, then, we need to recognize that divine love is more than, and is deeper than, an emotion. It is one feature or attribute of the divine nature of God that when fully established in us becomes one of several character-traits which make up the total character of the life of Christ which is in us.

God loves, yet not because He is affected by outside stimuli of various kinds, whether people or things. He simply loves because He *is* love. And because God cannot deny himself with respect to His nature, love automatically and quite naturally comes forth from within Him as one of the character-traits of His nature. And hence, in reading through the entire Bible we discover that one such trait of God's character is love—divine love.

Human Love (*Phileo*) and Divine Love (*Agape*)

Naturally speaking, we do not have this love in us. We instead have a kind of love which is actually a natural inclination. This kind of love is referred to in the Bible's New Testament original Greek as *phileo*, meaning that a person is naturally inclined to have some liking towards another person—in other words, friendship. We humans do know this kind of love; but as regards the love whose expression is independent of circumstances and other outside factors, that is a love we do not possess in and of ourselves. This latter kind of love is referred to in the New Testament's original Greek as *agape*—which is absolute, pure love. And only God possesses and exhibits that kind of love.

We often think we have that *agape* love. And we commence loving God and man with that love until one day we discover to our surprise that we simply do not have that love in us. Let us therefore recognize and acknowledge that if we are to have that love, it has to come from God.

Peter: Not an Example of *Agape* but *Phileo* Love

Let me use an illustration here. Peter thought he had great love for the Lord Jesus, and to some extent he did. On the evening of Jesus' betrayal and arrest He foretold to His disciples that they would all fall away from Him that night and how they would all be scattered in their attempting to save their lives. Peter declared in response that though all the other disciples might fall away, he would not; and further, he insisted that he would not deny the Lord and that he was willing to die with Him. But we know too well what happened when the time of testing that same night arrived. For Peter proceeded to deny the Lord three times.

I do believe that this disciple had been sincere in his vehement declaration of loyalty towards his Lord, that it was not empty words from his lips; he well meant his words at the time of uttering them, he believing he had that *agape* love in him. Peter discovered to his great surprise and sorrow, however, that he did not possess such love; and going out away from the place of his denial, Peter wept bitterly (Matthew 26:31-35, 57-58, 69-75).

However, not many days after Jesus' resurrection, He appeared one morning to some of His disciples, including Peter, when they were fishing on Lake Galilee (for this entire incident see John 21:1-17). And shortly later, as they were eating a breakfast which the Lord had prepared for them over a fire on the lakeshore, Jesus asked Peter, "Simon, son of Jonah, do you love Me more than these?" Now what did Jesus mean by "these"? In toto, the Lord was more than likely referring to the fire, the breakfast fish and bread, the boat and fishing net, and Peter's companions. "Do you, Peter, love Me more than the fire? Once, most recently, you showed openly that you loved the fire more than Me; for it was by the fire that you denied Me. You loved the warmth, the comfort and ease of life which that fire provided you more than you loved Me. Once, most recently, you loved your own life by having fled away from Me to save your own skin rather than continuing to identify yourself with Me. Once, you strove to be popular among your companions more than loving Me. So, I ask you, Simon son of Jonah, do you love Me more than these? Do you love Me with a pure, an absolute love?" And Peter, employing here the *phileo* term for love and not the *agape* term the Lord used in His question, could only answer, in so many words, as follows: "Lord, You know I am attached to You, that I have some feeling and inclination towards You; but You know that I cannot say that I *agape* You with anything close to a pure love for You." To which the Lord responded with: "Feed My lambs."

Again a second time Jesus inquired of Peter, "Simon, son of Jonah, do you love Me?" Here, without employing any comparison with other things, Jesus simply asked, "Simon, son of Jonah, do you love Me?" And Peter, by this time knowing himself better than in the recent past, replied, again in so many words, as follows, still using the term *phileo*: "Lord, You know that I love You, that I have a feeling towards You, that I am attached to You; but I cannot honestly bring myself to say that I love You absolutely. I know myself better now, and I acknowledge that I have fallen. But I can at least say that I have some inclination towards You and am attached to You." To which the Lord replied: "Shepherd My sheep."

Still a third time, Jesus—though now employing the *phileo* term for love—asked: "Simon, son of Jonah, do you love Me?— Are you at least attached to Me? Do you have some feeling and inclination towards Me?" Peter, grieved that the Lord had inquired of him a third time, and now greatly saddened by the fact that his Master had had to lower the love term from *agape* to *phileo*, realizing also that he in himself could not rise to the level of divine love, and that he today knew it was not in him, sadly replied,

"Lord, You know that I have some feeling of friendship towards You, that I am attached to You and cannot cut myself loose from You. You well know this about me, because You know me far better and far deeper." To which once more the Lord Jesus responded with, "Feed My sheep."

Agape Love Not Naturally in Us

I believe we can discern from this experience of Peter's that though we do have some degree of *phileo* love in us towards the Lord, we do not have the *agape* love. Rather, our love is more or less dependent upon the kinds of people around us and the circumstances surrounding us. The love within us is not the kind which is so strong that it is not affected by what is outside and around us. That love—even the *agape* love of our Father-God and of Christ Jesus—is not in us.

Yes, our love can love the lovely, but it cannot also love the unlovely. Such is beyond our capacity to love with an absolute, pure love; we cannot love for love's sake and for no other reason. When we love, there is a selfish reason behind it. Let us contrast that kind of love with God's *agape* love: He loves us with selflessness. For us to have this kind of love, it has to come from God. That is why the Bible declares that "love is of God, and every one who loves (the *agape* way) is born of God" (see I John 4:7b). Such love has to come from Him.

It is true that we do not have this love in us. There will come a day when we will need to acknowledge this. And probably the sooner we acknowledge it, the better. Otherwise, as we try to love, what comes out is our self: it is a counterfeit. We may deceive ourselves until one day we suddenly wake up to the fact that the *agape* love is just not in us but is simply our self coming forth. I therefore think that if we can realize this as early as possible, that will be a real blessing to us. It may be a shock, but it will be a blessing.

Nevertheless We *Do* Have *Agape* Love in Us

Having observed the above, however, I must quickly add that we *do* have this *agape* love in us. For in Romans 5 we read these reassuring words: that "the love of God has been poured out within our hearts through the Holy Spirit who was given to us" (v.5 NASB). We naturally do not have this love in us. But since we have believed in the Lord Jesus, we are now children of God; and as His children, He has poured out *His* love into our hearts by the Holy Spirit.

In other words, the indwelling Holy Spirit, who is the Spirit of Life, has brought to us a new life for ourselves, even the life of Christ; and one of the characteristics or traits of that life is love—even the *agape* love—which we did not have before we believed in the Lord Jesus.

Now if we learn to live by the life of Christ, one of whose character-traits is *agape* love, then that characteristic can begin to be developed in us, we now being able to love naturally and supernaturally. And as we continue to follow the Christ-life in us, His love shall become part of the character of Christ that is gradually being matured and more fully established in us day by day. And as has been noted before, this character-trait of love becomes one of the seven support pillars for the House of Rest and Peace—the glorious church—which Wisdom Personified, Christ Jesus, is building for God His Father.

Abiding in the Lord's Love: Keeping His Commandments

Before proceeding further, I would like to place before us for our consideration the following Scripture passage from John 15:

As the Father has loved me, I also have loved you: abide in my love. If ye shall keep my commandments, ye shall abide in my love, as I have kept my Father's commandments and abide in his love. I have spoken these things to you that my joy may be in you, and your joy be full. This is my commandment, that ye love one another, as I have loved you. No one has greater love than this, that one should lay down his life for his friends (vv. 9-13).

Herein do we see the Lord Jesus speaking to His disciples this precious word: "As the Father has loved Me, and I have loved you, you must abide in My love." The Father has loved the Son: that is a fact. Also, the Son, the Lord Jesus, has loved us: that, too, is a fact. Nothing can change these facts, which are eternal. And in our realizing these unchanging facts, now then, says the Lord Jesus to us, we must move forward into the experience of abiding in His love.

Has the Lord loved us? He has, and thus we do know His love. And to the extent that we know His love, to that extent shall be the love of God—the *agape* love—that flows forth from us. Why, we may ask, is this so? It is because the very source of *this* love in and out from us is God the Father and God the Son. We cannot find this *agape* love anywhere else than in our Father-God and in His Son, the Lord Jesus. And as we come to know this divine love, God's love commences to constrain us and so we begin to abide in His love. Indeed, we make His love our spiritual home. And as we make His love our home, we shall discover that we begin to love. To state this another way, if we are to love and have it developed and established in us, then, first of all, we will need to abide in the Lord's love. Only then does His love become our love. Otherwise, there is actually no *agape* love being developed in us that can flow forth from us.

One problem with us believers is this, that after we are saved we are told that we must love: love God, love our Christian brethren, and love the unbelievers in the world, including our enemies. Hence, since we are seriously instructed along this line of obligation, we strive to love all such—even our enemies. We try very hard to do so. And why? Because we desire to be good Christians. In trying, for instance, to love God, we may even tell Him, "Oh God, I love You, I love You very, very much." Nevertheless, should He subsequently reveal His mind to us along the line of that which is not pleasing to us or does not comport with our idea or desire, and so we reject or ignore God's speaking to us—where, then, is our love towards God?

Our love must not be merely in words and lips. It must be demonstrated otherwise. How, therefore, can we prove that our love is genuine towards the Lord? We find the answer in that same Scripture passage from John 15 quoted earlier. Jesus taught His disciples as follows: "You must keep My commandments as I have kept my Father's commandments. If you do that, then that obedience confirms that you love Me and the Father."

However, too often we consider God's commandments to be a heavy load, burdensome, and not pleasant. So, we fail to obey His commandments. And in the process it becomes clear to us that there is no love in us towards God. We end up loving Him only when everything is fine and pleasant, when He provides all things for us, and especially when it appears that He allows us to do whatever we like. But whenever God begins to indicate to us that which is contrary to our liking or desire, we instantly deem His requirements of us as being too hard and grievous. This kind of reaction on our part reveals the fact that there is actually no love of the *agape* kind in us.

It is only when we recall and are touched afresh by God's past love towards us, only when we are constrained by His love (cf. II Corinthians 5:14a), then His commandments are not hard, heavy, or burdensome. *Then*, it becomes our delight to do His will. And why? Because it is *His* love which is inspiring, encouraging and motivating us. It is in such pleasant circumstances as these that we find ourselves loving God; and therefore, His commandments are not heavy, harsh, unpleasant or disagreeable.

Loving Believers and Unbelievers

We think we love our brothers and sisters in the faith. Oh, we love everybody in the church! Fine. Oftentimes we are able to love someone who is a thousand miles away far better than the one who lives with us or nearby. Why is this the case? Because there is no rubbing up against others, but when we rub against one another, then, just see how much or little we can love our brothers and sisters in Christ.

One day Peter came to the Lord and said, "Now Lord, I have a brother, my brother Andrew, and he is such a good brother. However, he has sinned against me now these seven times, and I forgave him each time. Is that not good enough? Is that not the extent to which I am obligated to forgive my brother? Have I not therefore loved enough?" We see here that Peter's forgiving love had a limit: seven times. However, the Lord countered with this: "I do not say seven times but seventy times seven." He thus indicating that our forgiving love is to be limitless towards brethren who may sin against us (Matthew 18:21-22).

Yet, there was another occasion in which Jesus is found discussing with His disciples this same issue of forgiving one's brother in love. Said the Lord to them, that even should an offending brother have sinned against you seven times in one day (!) and should come to you after each of these seven times of wrongdoing and says that he repents, you must extend forgiving love to him all seven times. Again, we can infer from this that Jesus is once more indicating the limitlessness of our Christian obligation to forgive (Luke 17:3-4). Most interestingly, the disciples' response was not—as one might expect—"Give us more love," but was "Give more faith to us," or, as several other Bible translations have them exclaiming: "Increase our faith!" (v.5)

Like those first disciples of the Lord we, too, lack faith in our Christian brethren to believe them to be sincere when they tell us of their apology with the words, "I repent"—especially if they will have had to do this seven times in a single day! How, then, in such a situation, can we love them? Such *agape* love most surely has to come to us from God.

Have you ever found yourself in a circumstance wherein you are unable to love your brother or sister in the church assembly? No matter how hard you try, you cannot do so. Though you do not hate this or that brother or sister (you saying to yourself that at least such is good enough), you cannot love them.

There is a marked difference between liking and loving someone. We may not like a brother or sister, but the Lord does say we have to love them. He does not say that we must like somebody; this we do not find in the Bible. But we do find in Scripture that we are told by the Lord that we are to love everyone. Can we, though, love everybody? We must acknowledge that such is not in us, but that it must come from God. Oh, if we could love with brotherly-love! Why, in Scripture, is such love referred to as brotherly-love? It is because we are to love for one reason only: we and they are brothers and sisters in Christ: not for any other reason do we love one another.

Oftentimes our so-called Christian love has some other reason behind it in our "loving" this brother or that sister. What may that be? Well, it may be because our temperaments seem to fit or that we may have the same or similar interests; and so, we may like each other but we also "love" each other. Nevertheless, true brotherly-love of the *agape* kind has no distinction attached to it; it is not discriminating in favor of this brother or sister in the Lord or that brother or sister. Not so. We are to show *agape* love simply because the other person is a brother or a sister in Christ. And for this to actually occur, such love has to come from God; it just is not in us.

The same is true with respect to your loving the unbelievers in the world, or those who may become your enemies, or the people with whom you daily work. For instance, you may find it very difficult to love someone with whom you work closely in an office setting: that person may give you much trouble and many headaches. What are you going to do: can you love that individual, can you pray for that person? Let us recognize the fact that the love of God—even His *agape* love—is not natural to us; it has to come from Him, for it is a character-trait of the nature of the Christ-life which is now in us on the basis of our faith in the Lord Jesus. And so, we must go to the Lord and pray for Him to love through us all such people with whom we interact in our daily lives.

Love Covers a Multitude of Transgressions and Sins

Why love? According to Proverbs, "Love covereth all transgression" (10:12b). How can the church of God be built if there is no love? The building of the house of God is not a mechanical or technical work but is a spiritual work; and to build that house, love is essential. If there is no love, there can be no building because love covers all transgressions.

I think the best illustration in the Bible concerning this verse from Proverbs is what happened when Noah got drunk (Genesis 9:20-27). After the flood, Noah became a farmer and planted a vineyard, and so he had many grapes which he made into wine and proceeded one day to get drunk. Think of that! This righteous Noah got drunk, and because he was no longer conscious of what he was doing, Noah ended up uncovering himself and was now lying naked in his tent.

What then occurred was as follows. Although we cannot be certain, most likely the first person to have looked upon Noah's naked state was his grandson Canaan, since Noah, when afterwards he learned what certain of his progeny had done to him during his drunkenness, pronounced a curse not upon his son Ham but upon Ham's own son, Canaan (v.25). In view of this fact, therefore, evidently it was Canaan who was the first person who happened to come upon his grandfather's exposure, and who immediately went to his father Ham and reported—in what was probably a joking and laughing manner—what he had witnessed: "Oh, Grandfather got drunk, and I saw him naked—can you imagine that?!?" And Ham, in turn, apparently went eagerly to witness the sight himself (v.24b).

Moreover, we can again likely infer from the Genesis account that Ham, too, must have reacted in similar fashion to that of his son Canaan, since he himself made no attempt to cover his father's nakedness: "Look at that! My father has gotten so drunk that he has ended up lying there in his tent naked! Hmm … I well recall this father of ours disciplining us three brothers and telling us what we should and should not do; but now I cannot believe what I saw there in my father's tent!" And off went Ham to see his two brothers, Shem and Japheth, and told them about the matter in perhaps a gossiping, even jocular manner, and possibly with even great delight over his father's moment of weakness.

However, in great contrast to Ham's behavior, when Shem and Japheth heard what had happened to their father, they took an upper garment and placed it upon both their shoulders, walked backward towards the tent so as not to see their father's nakedness, and, upon entering Noah's tent, they let fall the garment upon their father's body, thus covering up his nakedness; and instantly thereafter they left the tent.

To me that episode serves as an excellent example of love sensitively expressed. However, too many times in our day, when we Christians are made privy to some faults, weaknesses, or shortcomings in our fellow church brethren, we do not express love. What is worse, we may even go forth and commence to broadcast the matter to others, and within perhaps an hour every brother and sister in the church will know about it; for we are aware, are we not, of how rapidly bad news and unpleasant rumors travel; for unfortunately, how we love to gossip! Is all such an expression of *agape* love? Hardly!

When people of the world get together, what do they generally talk about? The topics of their conversation usually revolve around the weather or politics or sports, etc. But when Christians come together, what is it which they talk about? About the Lord? No, the subject of their talking together too often turns out to be the faults and/or weaknesses and sins of their Christian brethren: "Oh! did you hear …? Have you heard what happened to brother or sister so-and-so? Oh, what a terrible thing he (or she) did!" In other words, we engage in gossip and spread news and possibly false rumors about our fellow believers without giving a moment's thought to what we are doing!

Is that love being manifested? According to the verse from Proverbs under discussion—"Love covereth all transgressions" —it definitely is not. This verse is not to be interpreted as meaning that love condones wrongdoing or sin, not at all; nor does it mean that love compromises with transgressions, equally not at all. Rather, the verse means that expressions of *agape* love attempt to cover in order to *recover* a fallen Christian. If, on the other hand, our response to those in the church with certain weaknesses is for us to broadcast them to others or engage in rumor-mongering, such may result in no recovery being possible. When love is sensitively expressed, it is meant to cover, not condone: first cover and then *re*-cover: recovering is the desired outcome. Hence, we come to see that in the book of Proverbs the expression of love is a vital character-trait to be valued, developed and increased in us. And why? Because it will cover a multitude of transgressions and sins.

Love vs. Envy

"A sound heart is the life of the flesh; but envy the rottenness of the bones" (Proverbs 14:30). Where there is love, our heart will be at peace with itself and with others; and the heart, in turn, will even quicken or give life to our body. Envy, however, will rot away our bones.

Suppose you are envious of someone, what will happen? The person you envy will probably one day suffer at your hands because of some action you may very well take against that individual in order to "bring him/her down." And, even should you *not* do anything to that person, yet, simply by your having envy of him (or her) shall take its toll of you yourself: it will "rot your bones"; which is to say, that that envy of yours will corrupt you.

Love, on the other hand, calms your heart, refreshes it, and is instrumental in even quickening your body with new life. Love, not envy, not only does good to others but also does good to yourself.

Love Dispenses Grace

People who show love also dispense grace; in fact, these two are closely related to each other. That verse in I John noted earlier declares that "God is love" (4:8b); and in the Gospel of John we are told that God's Son is "full of grace" (1:14c). Why is there this close relatedness in the Divine? It is because love is a character-trait of the divine nature which characterizes the Son of God; and where there is *agape* love—whether in the Lord Jesus or in any of His devoted disciples—there grace is bound to come forth.

Unfortunately, too many of us who are Christ's followers do not possess much grace. And why? Simply because we do not have much of His love in us. If, however, the love of God is being developed in us, we can be gracious towards others; indeed, as that attribute of love is being increased in us, we can be very gracious: we can dispense much more grace.

Hence, the book of Proverbs is right when it says that the person who loves pureness of heart has also grace upon the lips (22:11a). In other words, that person will let fall grace upon grace from his or her lips wherever that person may go. Moreover, this same verse goes on to say that the person who loves and possesses grace has a friend in the king (v.11b) and can thus stand before those in authority. Now since we Christians have Christ's divine nature in us, that nature's character-trait of love needs to be developed, sustained, and ever increased in us day by day.

What Love Is

What is love—*agape* love? There is one entire chapter devoted to it in the apostle Paul's First Corinthians epistle. We cannot delve into all of its descriptive details of love which this chapter covers; but there is one section of it whose translation by J. B. Phillips I particularly like. It is quite full of life, and it reads as follows:

> This love of which I speak is slow to lose patience—it looks for a way of being constructive. It is not possessive: it is neither anxious to impress nor does it cherish inflated ideas of its own importance. Love has good manners and does not pursue selfish advantage. It is not touchy. It does not keep account of evil or gloat over the wickedness of other people. On the contrary, it is glad with all men when truth prevails. Love knows no

limit to its endurance, no end to its trust, no fading of its
hope; it can outlast anything. It is, in fact, the one thing
that still stands when all else has fallen (13:4-8a).

The first quality of love which we find described in Paul's
love-chapter is that "love suffereth long, and is kind" (13:4c)—it
is long-suffering. Why is this an essential element in love? Because
the apostle is writing about love among the brethren in the
Christian assembly of believers. The church, the body of Christ,
is what is in view in the chapter immediately preceding the love-
chapter; and chapter 14 has in view the functioning aspect of the
body of Christ: how spiritual gifts are to operate and be exercised
in the body. Here, then, we have before us the body of Christ with
all its different members who are differently gifted according to
the Spirit's good pleasure and will (12:11 ASV). But before the
body's members can commence exercising these gifts for the
upbuilding together of the body, they need to have and express
the love of God towards one another.

Now as pointed out already, the first element of love so
necessary if the body's members are indeed to be built up together
is for the members to manifest the long-suffering quality of God's
love. God does not want the members of Christ's body to be
loosely related like the sand on the seashore but to be closely knit
in every way—in both spirit and soul. Only long-suffering love
can make this possible.

Of course, if we as body members only meet occasionally and
put forward our best "Sunday manner," then it is relatively easy
to be very polite, kind, and considerate towards one another.
However, if we as members of one body in Christ are intent on
being knitted together closely in spirit, then we shall discover over
time that there remains in us a great deal of rubbish belonging to
our flesh rather than it all being of Christ in us. Yes, we have
Christ in us whose life unites us together as His body; yet the old
Adamic flesh in each one of us tends to divide us.

No two persons are alike—not even twins. There will always
be some difference. How, therefore, can we as different members

of Christ's body be together as one and not be divided? How can we build up one another and not destroy one another? God's answer is: His divine love, whose first essential element is long-suffering patience and kindness. We have to be patient with one another: we must be slow, very slow, to lose patience. And that may involve much, much suffering. Nevertheless, if we are unable to suffer long in patience with one another, we will never learn to be kind and, in the words of the Phillips translation, to find "a constructive way" of helping one another.

As I see it, then, all the foregoing positive descriptions are a picture of true *agape* love.

Love Is the Fruit of the Spirit

Scripture tells us that love is the first of several fruits of God's Holy Spirit (Galatians 5:22a). This makes clear that love is not the result of any work or effort of ourselves but is the outgrowth of life. Hence, if we are filled with the Spirit of Life, then love shall naturally come forth as fruit.

How Love Is Developed

Thank God that the potential for His love to be expressed through us is definitely in us; for Christ's life is in us, and one attribute of that divine life in us is love. Why, however, is that *agape* love not being developed in many Christians today? We are told in history that what impressed the world most about the early church was the love which was present among her members. For the world would point to those earliest Christians and declare: "Oh! See how they love and care for one another!" How, then, can that same love of God be developed as an established feature which characterizes the church in our day? I would suggest that there are a few basic considerations which we continually need to bear in mind.

1. We need ever and always to acknowledge that the love we express must be of God and must come from God: it is not natural to us, though the potential to love as God loves is there, but the actual loving must be of God.

2. We must believe that though the divine love is indeed not natural to us, it is nonetheless supernaturally present with us and in us, since the Lord's life, one of whose attributes is love, is in us.

3. The reason many of us fail to live out the life of love that is in us is because we ourselves—our very self-life—stands in the way. Hence, the Lord Jesus has said that we who would be His followers must deny ourselves, take up our cross daily, and follow Him (Luke 9:23).

In His mercy God will allow different circumstances to appear in order to test us on this issue of the release of His life of love through us. According to the apostle Paul we—as "earthen vessels," that is to say, we as common glazed-over jars of hardened clay—have in us a "treasure," even the life of Christ (II Corinthians 4:7a); and one of the glorious attributes of that treasure is divine love. But because this treasure of Christ's life of love is bound up and imprisoned within us as vessels of hardened nonporous clay, the love of God cannot flow forth and bless the lives of needful others. God will therefore permit certain trials and difficulties of various kinds to surround us jars of hardened clay in order that these vessels of clay may be cracked open so that the character-trait of Christ's life of love may be released and expressed.

What often happens, however, is that we put up resistance to those various adverse circumstances—which God's Spirit has arranged—in our attempt to preserve intact the integrity of our entire being. We try to protect ourselves from whatever could wreck our sense of wholeness and completeness. In other words, we insist on facing all such circumstances head on in our attempt to maintain our personal integrity; but in so doing we harden ourselves that much more to these God-permitted difficulties and trials, we not realizing that God by the Holy Spirit has been employing various kinds of environments to cause these clay vessels of ours to be cracked open and broken before Him.

On this very point, let me place before us for our consideration Paul's highly descriptive words in II Corinthians 4 regarding God's ways of testing us and His desired outcome for doing so:

> ... we have this treasure in earthen vessels, so that the surpassing greatness of the power will be of God and not from ourselves; we are afflicted in every way, but not crushed; perplexed, but not despairing; persecuted, but not forsaken; struck down, but not destroyed; always carrying about in the body the dying of Jesus, so that the life of Jesus also may be manifested in our body. For we who live are constantly being delivered over to death for Jesus' sake, so that the life of Jesus also may be manifested in our mortal flesh. So death works in us, but life in you. (vv. 7-12 NASB).

From this passage we are given to understand that God will use environments of every kind to break open these clay vessels of ours and thus bring us to the point of seeing that He wishes us to let go of ourselves so that Christ's life of love can flow out and for us to look to the Lord and pray: "Lord, if You want me to love, You will have to do it, since I myself cannot." And to our surprise, He does it, because—as the apostle dramatically explained it—"the surpassing greatness of the power [is] of God and not from ourselves." Let me stress, however, that for this outcome to occur it will involve an ongoing process wherein we must deny our self-life, take up our cross, and follow the Lord.

If we continue on with God in this manner, we shall gradually discover that His love as one of the character-traits of the nature of Christ's life in us has become a trait of our character, too. At the beginning of this process we shall most likely need to experience death and resurrection multiple times: the denying of self and the taking up of our cross; but then, the experiencing of the power of Christ's resurrection with regard to God's love. Hence, over time we shall increasingly discover that we are able to love as God loves, and to do so unconsciously. In fact, loving as God himself loves will have become so supernaturally natural to us that that flow of His love has now become an established trait of our own character. And when that happens, we shall no longer be conscious of loving anyone.

It can therefore rightly be observed that in the process of love being developed in us in the manner just described we at the beginning are conscious of loving, which is indicative of the fact that our loving as God loves has not yet become that substantial in us; but as we eventually become unconscious of loving and yet that love is spreading forth and being dispensed out from us, at that moment God's love has become established as a matured character-trait in us. And it is this character-trait in God's people with which Christ is building His church that shall ultimately become God's House of Rest and Peace on earth.

May God be gracious and most merciful to us.

> Lord, Thou hast greatly encouraged us, because even though love is not naturally in us, and yet, Thou dost show that Thou hast miraculously put Thy love in us by having shed abroad in our hearts Thy great love. And Lord, we want to know more of this love. We do desire to give ourselves to Thee and to let Thee live out Thy love through us. O Lord, we thank Thee for bringing us many times to a point in our lives where we cannot love anymore. We have come to our limit, but we do praise and thank Thee that Thou art the infinite God whose love is limitless. So, Lord, may Thou thyself be increasing in us and may Thou increase this Thy love in all of us. Oh, may Thy church be characterized by love so that Thy church may be built—to the praise of Thy glory. In Thy precious name we ask. Amen.

Pillar 4—The Character-Trait of Lowliness

Proverbs 11:2—When pride cometh, then cometh shame; but with the lowly is wisdom.

Proverbs 13:10—By pride there only cometh contention; but with the well-advised is wisdom.

Proverbs 14:29—He that is slow to anger is of great understanding; but he that is hasty of spirit exalteth folly.

Proverbs 15:25—Jehovah plucketh up the house of the proud; but he establisheth the boundary of the widow.

Proverbs 16:5—Every proud heart is an abomination to Jehovah: hand for hand, he shall not be held innocent ["hand for hand" means certainly—per Darby note].

Proverbs 16:18—Pride goeth before destruction, and a haughty spirit before a fall.

Proverbs 16:19—Better is it to be of a humble spirit with the meek, than to divide the spoil with the proud.

Proverbs 18:12—Before destruction the heart of man is haughty; and before honour goeth humility.

Proverbs 21:4—Lofty eyes, and a proud heart, the lamp of the wicked, is sin.

Proverbs 21:24—Proud, arrogant, scorner is his name who dealeth in proud wrath.

Proverbs 22:4—The reward of humility and the fear of Jehovah is riches, and honour, and life.

Proverbs 29:23—A man's pride bringeth him low; but the humble in spirit shall obtain honour.

We come now to the fourth Pillar of Wisdom, which is the character-trait of Lowliness. The words "lowly" and "humble" appearing in the above passages in Proverbs mean the same thing.

Lowliness means to lie low, to empty oneself, to take a low place, to think nothing of oneself, not to try to exalt oneself, not to try to take advantage in order to promote oneself. The very opposite of lowliness is pride. Pride means haughtiness in spirit, exalting oneself, puffing up, trying to put everyone underneath oneself.

Jesus the Example of Lowliness

Lowliness is more than an action. There must also be a disposition or attitude of humility behind the act. Sometimes a person may seem to act in a lowly way, but that does not necessarily mean that that person has a lowly or humble disposition. While on earth Jesus was lowly and meek in heart. When one thinks of lowliness, one cannot help but think of Him because His spirit was that of lowliness. In the Philippians epistle of Paul's we are told that though the Lord Jesus is equal with God (which was not something for Him to hold onto because He is himself the Son of God and is therefore one with God), He nonetheless emptied himself of such attributes of Deity as glory and honor, and took upon himself the form of a slave and in the likeness of a man; moreover, He humbled himself towards God by becoming obedient even unto death, and that the death of the cross (2:6-8). The very spirit of Christ is lowliness. In fact, He said this: "Take my yoke upon you and learn from me; for I am meek and lowly in heart; and ye shall find rest to your souls" (Matthew 11:29).

Lowliness: Not in Us by Nature

The spirit of Christ is lowliness, but lowliness or humility is not an aspect of our natural character. It is natural in fallen man to be proud, arrogant, and haughty. You may think that if you have nothing, surely you would be lowly and not proud. But the paradox of life is such that the less you have, the prouder you become. Or else you have to put up some front or façade to make you feel good. You cannot afford to be lowly or to be humble. Why? Because if you do, that means you are a nobody. It is only the one who has much who is able to be lowly and to be meek. Lowliness is not a weakness as we often think; rather, lowliness is strength. It is only those who have strength who are able to be meek and lowly and humble, because they can afford to be so. First of all, then, we have to see that lowliness is not in us naturally.

The Fall of Lucifer and Mankind through Pride

A crucial problem in the universe is to be found surrounding the issue between pride and lowliness or meekness. Consider especially, in this regard, the fall of the archangel, Lucifer. God had created him with such beauty and such talents and had placed him in such a high position: Lucifer was the anointed cherub that covered the throne of God. Yet pride had eventually entered his heart, for he was not content to be under God: he was above all other angels, but was still under God: nevertheless, he ultimately wanted to be equal with God; and because of this, the spirit of pride eventually entered into him. Indeed, it turned Lucifer into the devil. It was not God who made Lucifer the devil. Lucifer made a devil out of himself (Isaiah 14:12-15, cf. Ezekiel 28:1ff.).

Let us also consider mankind. When God created the first man, Adam, mankind was innocent. And as we know, God put Adam in the Garden of Eden and made every provision for him there. Adam was free, God told him, to eat the fruit from any and all the Garden's trees except, he commanded, from the tree of the knowledge of good and evil, because on the day that he would eat of the fruit from that tree, he would surely die (Genesis 2:16-17). On the one hand, this specific prohibition was actually an expression of the love of God; and on the other hand, this commandment of God's would serve to remind Adam that though he had been placed above all non-human things on the earth, he was nonetheless under the authority of God.

But oh how Adam's wife, Eve, was tempted! How was she tempted? Eve beheld the tree, and while she was gazing at it, which she acknowledged to herself was good in several ways, she was told by the serpent-devil that if she would eat of this tree's fruit she would become as wise as God. "Oh," thought Eve, "if eating of this tree's fruit can make me as intelligent and wise as God, I (and my husband) will not need to be under God anymore, since we will be equal to Him." So she took of this tree's fruit, ate, and gave some of it to Adam (Genesis 3:1-6). This act was nothing other than "the pride of life" written about long afterwards by Jesus' apostle John (I John 2:16). Here was no expression of a spirit of lowliness but was the manifestation of a proud, arrogant, disobedient spirit. And such ushered in the Fall of mankind.

Man thus rebelled against God because there was now pride in him. And such is a root of all kinds of sin. Accordingly, after the Fall of man we who were born of Adam inherited Adam's life. We inherited that old nature of his, and in that old nature we do not find lowliness or humility there but instead we find pride, arrogance, and haughtiness in the very being or makeup of man.

We shall often be surprised to learn that those whom we may assume have nothing about which to be proud turn out to be the proudest people! That is simply human nature being exhibited. Do not assume that you have been born as a humble, meek, or lowly and gentle person. You may appear to be possessed of that kind of spirit; but just you wait till someone touches you the wrong way and then observe what will happen to you! One of Solomon's wise sayings declares that "by pride there only cometh contention, anger and strife" (Proverbs 13:10a). Indeed, pride brings in anger and destruction (16:18, cf. 14:29a).

Losing Our Temper through Pride

I recall that brother Watchman Nee once gave a message on losing one's temper. He inquired: What is the reason which lies behind a person losing his temper? It is basically the matter of one's pride. When your pride is touched, challenged, or is being "stepped on," you lose your temper. Brother Nee went on to observe that losing your temper is simply your way of preserving your pride and protecting yourself. Lowliness is simply not in us. First of all, then, we must acknowledge that lowliness or humility is not our natural state or condition. Yet, though we ourselves lack that, it *is* in the spirit of Christ. And hence, if this character-trait is

90

to be manifested and expressed in and through us, it will have to come from the Lord whose very nature has within it the attribute of lowliness and meekness.

It is very evident that by nature we fallen humans do not have humility or lowliness in us. Consider Jesus' twelve disciples. When they were called they left everything to follow the Lord. They loved Him to such an extent that they were willing to forsake all things in order to be attached to Him. So, they must certainly have been a beautiful people—right?—for they had given up so much just to follow the Lord. So, they must have been very spiritual, right? Yet these same disciples had quarreled several times among themselves as to who was the greatest among them! Every one of them had wanted to be considered the greatest (Matthew 18:1-5; Mark 9:33-37; Luke 9:46-48, 22:24). They had known nothing of humility nor lowliness; instead, it could rightly be said that at that time there was among them a spirit of haughtiness and pride.

Even on the occasion when Jesus, nearing the end of His earthly ministry, had shared with the Twelve what was to happen to Him concerning His soon crucifixion, they were still arguing among themselves as to who was the greatest in their group. Let us in fact recall what was Jesus' reaction to their quarreling about this matter on this same occasion. All three synoptic Gospels inform us somewhat differently with regard to various details; even so, they all state that Jesus took a small child and placed it in their midst, and, according to Matthew's account, He said the following:

> Truly, truly, I say to you all, Unless you are converted and become as little children, you will in no way enter the kingdom of the heavens. Whoever therefore shall humble himself as this little child, the same is the greatest in the kingdom of the heavens (see 18:3-4).

Unfortunately, at this moment, the Twelve did not learn the lesson which the Lord had intended for them to learn.

We know this observation to have been true of the Twelve because of how these same disciples conducted themselves during the beginning moments of their last Passover feast which they subsequently experienced with their Lord as a family on the very night of His betrayal (and recorded in John 13:1-15). Briefly stated, the following description can set the scene for what happened during those opening moments of their time together.

Upon their entering the Upper Room of a particular Jerusalem home, these disciples noticed that all was ready for celebrating the Passover together, except for one detail: no servant-maid was present who would be tasked to wash their feet. The maid's basin was there, the pitcher of water was there, the towel was there, and all the food was there on the feast table—*but no maid!* It is my belief that the Lord Jesus had prearranged this one lack, in that I believe He had told His hosts, "Prepare all things necessary, but please do not have a servant-maid present upon our arrival," since, He had probably thought to himself, He wished to teach His disciples one last time a very important lesson.

We need to understand that according to the Jewish custom of that day, when anyone entered a home to enjoy a feast, that person would expect to have his feet washed first in order for him to be able to enjoy the feast refreshed. Hence, when the Twelve entered the room and noticed no servant-maid was present, they must have looked at one another in dismay. No servant present? What a terrible mistake their hosts had made! So, quite reluctantly, they all assumed their reclining places around the feast table; and although they all must have felt uncomfortable when doing so, not one among them did anything in an attempt to rectify the embarrassing situation. Meanwhile, their Master had been observing His disciples intently, and, with perhaps a mixture of amusement, disappointment and sadness, He finally took His own place at the table.

Now because nothing further happened during the next few moments, the Lord rose up, laid aside His outer garment, girded himself with the towel, poured water into the basin, and began to wash His disciples feet one by one. Naturally, in order to wash someone's feet, a person must assume a very low position: one must kneel and then bow down quite low physically. And that was why none of the Twelve had wanted to be the one to take that lowly position. Whereas each of them felt that he was too worthy to perform such a humble and servile task, their Master and Lord had no hesitation in kneeling and bowing down low before His disciples to wash their feet. And upon completing this lowly service Jesus once again reclined at table with the Twelve. But He then said to them:

> Do you know what I have just now done to you? You call Me both Lord and Teacher, and you say rightly; for so in fact I am. If I, then, your Lord and Teacher have washed your feet, you also ought to wash one another's feet. For I have given you an example, in order that you also should do as I have done to you (see John 13:12-15).

This entire event was a lesson in love which Jesus the Master was teaching His disciples. For as the apostle John would much later inform the readers of his Gospel account of this episode, he wrote the following introductory words explaining what the Lord was about to do at this last Passover feast with His disciples: "Jesus, … having loved His own who were in the world, loved them to the end. And during [the Passover] supper, … Jesus rose up … and began to wash the disciple's feet …" (see 13:1c, 2a, 4a, 5b). It was, indeed, a lesson in love but also a lesson in lowliness, since one of the elements which constitute divine love and makes it possible to express that love is lowliness and humbleness.

How We Can Be Humble

Thus we have come to see that even towards the very end of Jesus' time on earth, His disciples, by their behavior, revealed the fact that humbleness in heart was not a quality in their character, nor is that the case with any of us. The Lord Jesus had been attempting to develop His character in the Twelve back then, and our Lord is attempting to accomplish the same objective in us today. God the Father wants very much to have His Son's character in all its attributes—including that of humbleness—produced in us. How does He go about achieving this? I believe it can come about through the combination of two undertakings: one by the Holy Spirit and the other by our Father-God by means of His Spirit.

The Illumination of the Holy Spirit

We have the life of Christ in us, and this new life of His is a lowly, humble life; in other words, Christ's life has lowliness in its very nature. Therefore, as we walk with the Lord, the Holy Spirit within us shall from time to time illumine us. The Holy Spirit who dwells in us will now and then teach us, expose us, and reveal our true selves to us.

The first reason we have no lowliness is that we do not know ourselves, and the second reason is that we do not know God. The only way to know ourselves is to know God, since "in His light we shall see light" (see Psalm 36:9b). We cannot see ourselves without the illuminating light of God; because without Him as our light, whenever we see ourselves, we see ourselves as being more than we really are, and also as being less than we really are. We see ourselves more glorious than we actually are, since we always harbor high thoughts of ourselves. Yet, the Bible teaches us "not to be high-minded" (Romans 11:20b, I Timothy 6:17a). Unfortunately, we think of ourselves more than we truly are in the sight of God. But the more we know God by letting His light shine more and more upon ourselves, that much more shall we be exposed by God and thus we begin to know ourselves accurately.

Take, for example, the Old Testament patriarch, Job. Job was a perfect man: upright, God-fearing, and fervent in every sense of the word. Nevertheless, there was one characteristic in Job which was wrong: pride. He was proud about his being perfect; so much so, that he could not tolerate people who would argue with him that he was *not* perfect. For when one of his three friends approached Job during his very personal crisis and said to him, "The reason you are suffering so much is because there must be some secret sin in you, and it must be a huge sin, at that; and hence, you are not perfect as you say you are"—Job became very angry.

Especially did Job explode in anger at his friends when they together counseled him that because of that hidden, grievous sin of his, he should confess to God this error. Job's three friends, of course, had greatly misunderstood him, for he did not harbor any secret sin. Until this moment, Job had been bearing most patiently his great loss of family, possessions, and untold physical pains and sufferings. But when his friends had begun falsely accusing him of his imperfection and declaring that he was not as perfect as he had thought of himself, this noble patriarch broke out in great anger, lost his temper, and claimed aloud: "I am perfect; I know I am perfect! If only God were here, I would stand before Him and demand that He show me where I am imperfect, if that in fact be the case!" We see here an expression by Job of self-righteousness and immense pride in his assumed perfection (see for friend Eliphaz: Job 4:7a, 8, 22:23; for Bildad: 8:20, 6; and for Zophar: 20:4a, 5, 11:4, 6c—all ASV).

Let us notice, however, that God did not argue with Job. Instead, He simply proceeded to reveal himself to Job. And upon this revelatory illumination of God by God to Job, His servant had to acknowledge to Him the following: "At one time I had heard of You, but now I have *seen* You, oh God; and I therefore confess to You that heretofore I had been proud, but no longer can I be so. I therefore abhor myself and repent in dust and ashes because I have sinned" (see re: God: Job 13:4, 19:2-3, 21, 23:3-9, 38:2-4, 40:9-12a, 14; and re: Job's response to God: 40:3-5, 42:1-6—all ASV).

Let us all understand that if we have only heard of God, we can easily be proud, indeed. But when we finally *see* who our God is, we can begin to know ourselves as we truly are. Humility and lowliness can only come from seeing God. And once we truly see Him, we commence accurately knowing who we ourselves truly are. And even after seeing God, if we still attempt to be proud, such pride cannot be worked up anymore, for that negative experience can be likened to a tire's inner tube which has been punctured: the air having escaped, the tube now lies totally flattened out.

How can we be of a lowly and meek spirit? We need the illumination of the Holy Spirit regarding our God. The Holy Spirit will bring to us from time to time a revelation of God, and in that light, we shall begin to see ourselves. In short, it will humble us.

The Father's Discipline through the Spirit's Arrangement of Circumstances

Now whereas the Holy Spirit's illuminating work constitutes one side of God's objective of developing in us a lowly and meek spirit, there is another and equally important side. That other side is our Father-God's discipline of us through the Spirit's arrangement of circumstances in our lives by which our pride can be deflated to the point of extinction and replaced by His Son's character-trait of lowliness and meekness. It is not only that the Holy Spirit who dwells in us will teach us and reveal our Father-God to us so that we are humbled before Him; but the Holy Spirit will also so arrange our circumstances in order to humble us, and sometimes to humiliate us. Since we are so proud in our nature, God wants to work His Son's lowliness in us. How does He do it? He by His Spirit has to raise up circumstances by which we must go through certain experiences that in some cases may be highly humiliating. The one experience we hate and wish to avoid above all is to be humiliated. Nevertheless, there are times when God must allow us to be humiliated for the purpose of humbling us; for He knows that if we are not humiliated, we shall refuse to be humble.

The Lord Jesus is so humble that He is *beyond* being humiliated. But we are *not* beyond being humiliated. We need to be humiliated occasionally. It can be a most painful experience, and so we fight against it: we resist it and resent it and get angry if such comes our way; for we do not ever want to be humiliated. But if in our experience we are never beyond humiliation, our humility is in question.

People can put the Lord Jesus on the cross and attempt to humiliate Him further, but by this time He is beyond being humiliated. Nor is the Lord affected by evil designs of any kind.

People may also attempt to mock Him by crying out at Him: "If you are the Son of God, come down from that cross of yours, and then we'll believe you!" Though they attempted to humiliate Him more and more, yet the Lord accepted it all with a spirit of humbleness. We are reminded, are we not, by what the Bible has observed, that if anyone "humbles himself under the mighty hand of God He will exalt that one in due time" (see I Peter 5:6). And that is precisely what God's Son experienced while on the cross; for when people attempted to humiliate Jesus further, He made no effort to speak or say anything to vindicate himself but simply humbled himself under His Father's mighty hand, saying, "Father, into thy hands I commit my spirit" (Luke 23:46a); and in due time, the Lord Jesus was "highly exalted" (Philippians 2:9a).

We need to realize that nothing happens to us by accident. Let us not blame others as though they have brought various situations on us. By outward appearance it may seem as though they have done so. No, it is the Holy Spirit who has been arranging all our circumstances in order to bring us into humility. The humility of God's Son is to be organized and developed in us. And during that organizing process there is bound to be discomfort and pain. Indeed, it is none other than the growing pain of spiritual life. Oh, if we can see and understand this, we shall be able to discern the love of the Father, even in the most adverse situations.

Our Father-God is waiting to establish His beloved Son's character-trait of lowliness in our heart and spirit, such that, we are able and sincerely willing to acknowledge: "I am nothing and can do nothing in this regard; in fact, I take no account of myself. Indeed, I can afford for my very self to be neglected, even forgotten." I recall, in this regard, what Andrew Murray once observed: "What is humility? It is not a thinking less of yourself. No, humility is not thinking of yourself at all." Frequently we may assume that to be humble means that we are to think less of ourselves in that because we may think we are someone great, therefore, for us to be humble we are to try thinking less of ourselves. However, what happens is that as we attempt to think less of ourselves, we are actually continually reminding ourselves that we think less of ourselves. But being humble simply means that we do not think of ourselves at all. In short, humility is simply selflessness. And it is this character-trait of God's Son which is what our heavenly Father is desirous of producing in us by means of His Spirit's wise arranging-activity.

The Subject of Lowliness in the New Testament

In the book of Proverbs we find that to be lowly is wisdom (11:2). To the lowly there is honor, riches, and life (18:12, 22:4, 29:23). Pride is an abomination in the sight of God (16:5). Pride comes before destruction, haughtiness before a fall (16:18), but whoever is lowly is wise. Now not only do we find this well-advised sentiment expressed in the Old Testament Proverbs, in the New Testament as well we are exhorted often to be lowly. For instance, of the many Beatitudes spoken by Jesus in His so-called Sermon on the Mount, the first one reads: "Blessed are the poor in spirit, for theirs is the kingdom of the heavens" (Matthew 5:3). It is in our spirit where humility and lowliness are to be found. It is not that we have nothing in our spirit, but that because we have much there, we can be poor in spirit. We are happy and blessed, because the kingdom of the heavens is ours.

As was pointed out earlier, Jesus illustrated this matter of humility and lowliness by means of placing a small child in the presence of His disciples and declaring to them this: "Unless you become as this little child, you cannot enter the kingdom of the heavens. He who humbles himself as this little child is the greatest in the kingdom of the heavens" (see Matthew 18:3-4). I hope this word of our Lord will register in us deeply.

In Romans chapter 12 we are exhorted by the apostle Paul as follows: "Be of the same mind toward one another; do not be haughty in mind, but associate with the lowly. Do not be wise in your own estimation" (v.16 NASB). Learn to be lowly and not to be high-minded, as if all others are beneath you and your dignity. Be with those of lowly estate; and do not be wise in your own eyes.

Paul also wrote this: "I, the prisoner in the Lord, exhort you therefore to walk worthy of the calling wherewith ye have been called, with all lowliness and meekness, with longsuffering, bearing with one another in love; using diligence to keep the unity of the spirit in the uniting bond of peace" (Ephesians 4:1-3). Lowliness is not only the secret for the obtaining of God's blessing, spiritual riches, honor, and life; it is also the secret for being united with our brothers and sisters. How can we maintain the unity of the Spirit? By expressing genuine lowliness and meekness. That, indeed, is the secret for being knitted together and joined together into one.

In Colossians chapter 3 the same sentiment is being exhorted by the apostle: "Put on therefore, as the elect of God, holy and beloved, bowels of compassion, kindness, lowliness, meekness, long-suffering; forbearing one another, and forgiving one another, if any should have a complaint against any; even as the Christ has forgiven you, so also do ye" (vv. 12-13). Lowliness and meekness are once again brought into view as those traits of character, among others, for brethren in Christ to have in order for them to be united into one.

And the apostle Peter also exhorts the saints along the same line: "Likewise ye younger, be subject to the elder, and all of you bind on humility towards one another; for God sets himself against the proud, but to the humble gives grace." What is God's attitude towards the proud? He sets himself against them. What is God's attitude towards those who are humble? To them He gives grace; that is to say, He gives himself. Peter goes on to give wise counsel to all of us: "Humble yourselves therefore under the mighty hand of God, that he may exalt you in the due time; having cast all your care upon him, for he cares about you" (I Peter 5:5-7).

Hence, we are exhorted to learn to be humble; but as I have pointed out several times, we cannot in and of ourselves accomplish this. We may try to be humble. We may even hunch our backs and put forth great effort to be humble, but in our hearts we rise that much higher up in our own estimation. Please be advised once again that being humble is not a matter of our trying to perform an outward humble act. That is not what is meant by being lowly. It instead is a matter of inward character. The life of Christ in us is a lowly and meek life; and if we learn to walk with Him and are willing to accept the dealings of the cross in our lives, then the Holy Spirit will do His part—whatever is required—to develop and increase in us Christ's character-trait of lowliness until we ourselves are distinguished inwardly by this attribute of lowliness.

However, in this organizing and developing process by the Holy Spirit, we cannot pretend; the desired outcome must be of Christ and not of ourselves. And when lowliness has become our inward disposition, we shall not even think of lowliness. For let us be aware that if we have to think of being lowly, then there has not been that particular character-trait developed in us yet. But whenever we do not even think about being lowly but its expression comes forth quite supernaturally naturally, then it can rightly be said that lowliness has become a disposition and character-trait in us.

Finally, let us not forget that this attribute of lowliness constitutes one of the seven pillars which Christ desires to have in support of the House of Rest and Peace which He is building for God the Father.

May the Lord have mercy upon us.

Our heavenly Father, we do praise and thank Thee that Thou hast put Thy Son's life in us. And the very nature of that life can be described as being humble, lowly, and meek. Oh Father, how we praise and thank Thee that there is the potential in us, and we do desire to see that the nature of Thy Son's life is being developed into a character quality which distinguishes us. But Father, Thou hast to do it. We simply hand ourselves over to Thee, and pray that Thou wilt illumine us from within, and that Thou wilt discipline us from without. We are willing to deny ourselves by Thy grace, take up our cross, and follow Thy Son, and allow Him to work himself in us and out from us. And to Thee be all the praise and the glory. In the name of our Lord Jesus. Amen.

Pillar 5—The Character-Trait of Graciousness

Proverbs 11:16—A gracious woman retaineth honour; and the violent retain riches.

Proverbs 11:17—The merciful man doeth good to his own soul; but the cruel troubleth his own flesh.

Proverbs 11:25—The liberal soul [Lit., The blessing soul—per Darby note] shall be made fat, and he that watereth shall be watered also himself.

Proverbs 14:21—He that despiseth his neighbour sinneth; but he that is gracious to the afflicted, happy is he.

Proverbs 14:31—He that oppresseth the poor reproacheth his Maker; but he that honoureth Him is gracious to the needy.

Proverbs 15:4—Gentleness of tongue is a tree of life; but crookedness therein is a breaking of the spirit.

Proverbs 19:11—The discretion of a man maketh him slow to anger, and it is his glory to pass over a transgression [or, over an offense—per Darby note].

Proverbs 19:17—He that is gracious to the poor lendeth unto Jehovah; and what he hath bestowed will he repay unto him.

Proverbs 19:22—The charm of a man is his kindness; and a poor man is better than a liar.

Proverbs 20:28—Mercy and truth preserve the king; and he upholdeth his throne by mercy.

Proverbs 22:9—He that hath a bountiful eye shall be blessed, for he giveth of his bread to the poor.

The fifth Pillar of Wisdom in support of God's House of Rest and Peace which Christ who is Wisdom Personified is building for His Father is the Lord's character-trait of Graciousness. There are various words which have been employed in the above-quoted proverbs which more or less convey the same thought: words such as gracious, merciful, liberal, bountiful, gentle, and kind. For our purpose here I have simply grouped together the above-selected relevant wise sayings in Proverbs having to do with this fifth Pillar of Wisdom which I have called Christ's character-trait of Graciousness.

Our God is One who is full of grace, and He is therefore a most gracious God. Early on in their wilderness experience the Israelites had sinned greatly against Jehovah God. So Moses ascended back up the Sinai desert mount once more to plead with God on behalf of these disobedient people; and God forgave them. He then told Moses to carve out two new stone tablets, bring them to Him, and He would once again inscribe His basic Law, the Ten Commandments, upon these two new tables of stone (Exodus 32:30-34:4). And having done this, God subsequently proceeded to make to Moses the following declaration:

> **Jehovah, Jehovah God, merciful and gracious, slow to anger and abundant in goodness and truth, keeping mercy unto thousands, forgiving iniquity and transgression and sin, but by no means clearing the guilty; visiting the iniquity of the fathers upon the children, and upon the children's children, and upon the third and upon the fourth generation (Exodus 34:6-7).**

From this we see that He is indeed a most gracious God.

Let us recall that the New Testament Gospel of John makes a similar declaration concerning the coming into this world of God's Son, the Lord Jesus Christ: "And the Word became flesh and tabernacled among mankind, being full of grace and truth" (see 1:14). We are thus given to know that, like Jehovah God, His Son, too, is very gracious. And because He is so gracious towards us, He requires of us who are His followers to be gracious also. Even so, we must acknowledge that the attribute of graciousness is not in fallen mankind.

Now it is because of this lack in man that Jesus needed to instruct His disciples in this matter of being gracious. For instance, one day His disciple Peter came to the Master and, in so many words, said the following to Him: "Lord, my brother has sinned against me these seven times, and on each occasion I had forgiven him. Is that not enough?" For Peter, that was quite an achievement, given his impulsive, quick-tempered, impatient personality. And more than likely this disciple had become very proud of himself over this achievement; and hence, he probably came to the Lord in this frame of mind and thinking that Jesus would agree with him that forgiving seven times is certainly enough. The Lord, however, replied, saying: "You must forgive not just seven times but seventy times seven"; thus connoting the idea of an infinite number of times one must forgive (see Matthew 18:21-22).

Jesus then employed a most dramatic parable by which to teach His disciple on the necessity of exercising graciousness. Now in the parable a king was found to have loaned one of his bondslaves what, in American currency, would amount to some ten million dollars. And when there came the time of reckoning, the king demanded repayment from his bondslave, and if the slave was not able, the king threatened to sell him, his wife, his children, and all possessions he had. Falling down low in homage to the king, the slave begged and pleaded with the king to be merciful and show him patience and he would eventually repay all the loan. At this point the king, who of course knew his slave could not make good on the debt, was so moved with compassion that he forgave his bondslave the entire massive debt and released him.

Upon leaving the king's presence, however, this bondslave searched out a certain fellow bondslave who owed him a debt of only some twenty dollars. Seizing the debtor by the throat, he demanded immediate payment. In response, that fellow slave fell down at his feet and begged his creditor to be patient with him and he would repay the loan. But he refused and had him cast into prison. The king, having been told by his other bondslaves what had occurred, summoned this wicked slave of his and said: "Did

I not show you compassion, in response to your plea for mercy, and forgave you that huge debt of yours? Should you not therefore have had compassion on your fellow bondslave?" And the king, now extremely angry, cast this wicked slave into prison till he should repay the huge debt he had owed the king (see vv.23-35).

Like the king in the parable, our God is so gracious towards us; therefore, He expects us—those who are His people—to be merciful and gracious towards others, too. Otherwise, we will never be like Him. What characterizes our God and His Son ought to characterize us as well. Nevertheless, I must observe once again that grace is not natural to us; in fact, it is that which we do not know; it is foreign to us. In short, graciousness is not a character-trait of ours.

In this very connection we must hark back to the very beginning of mankind in the Garden of Eden. After the first man, Adam, and his wife had sinned, God had inquired of Adam, "What is this that you have done?" In response, this first man in human history explained in defense: "It was the woman whom You had given to be with me who ate the fruit of the forbidden tree and gave some to me and I ate" (see Genesis 3:11b-12). We can discern from this that there was no graciousness in Adam. Instead, he became selfish after having sinned against God's commandment: self-preservation immediately became an essential instinct in mankind; for to protect himself, this first man, now fallen, placed the blame for his disobedience on his wife. Adam did not have the slightest knowledge what graciousness is. In considering this historic episode we come to realize that in fallen mankind there is no trait of graciousness to be found.

In contrast to this sorry behavior, God's Son is most gracious, indeed. For upon our believing in Him He gives us His life whose very nature is marked by graciousness. And so, we who have Christ's life in us have this new nature of His, one of whose noble traits of character is that of graciousness. Having within us this trait in embryonic form, it needs to be developed so that it can be lived out from us in practical expression towards others. And by it ultimately arriving at its final form of development in us it will become in us a fully-established part of the multi-faceted character of Christ.

What Grace Is

What is grace? Grace has about it three interrelated aspects, the knowledge of which will enable us to have a proper understanding and appreciation of the true nature of grace.

The Source of Grace

In the first place grace is that which is within a person and which brings pleasure, delight and satisfaction to others who have contact with that person. It is not unlike the experience one has of looking at a beautiful picture or painting which causes there to rise up within that one a deep sense of pleasure and delight. And yet, it is obvious that the source of that delight lies not in the onlooker but in the picture or painting. And hence, the source of grace is to be found in the person whose inner nature prompts delight and satisfaction to arise in others. Such, then, is the first aspect of grace.

The Giving of Grace Freely, Universally, and Without Repayment

Now because that person is full of grace which quite naturally provides others with a sense of delight and pleasure and satisfaction, it can therefore be said that the person gives forth to others *freely*, gives forth to others *universally* without regard to their identity, and gives forth to others with no thought of *reciprocity* or repayment whatsoever. And such constitutes the second aspect or element about grace.

The Reproducing of Grace

Furthermore, as that grace is being offered freely, universally, and without required repayment, such gracious action produces in the recipient a heart of thankfulness; moreover, it also imparts to that recipient a disposition of wanting to be gracious, too. In other words, grace imparted reproduces itself in the recipient; and that forms the third interrelated aspect of grace.

Grace: Its Beginning and Continued Existence on Earth Only Found in Christ

Strictly speaking, the Lord Jesus Christ is grace; in fact, He is grace incarnate; for the Gospel of John informs us that though "the Law was given through Moses, grace subsists in Jesus Christ himself" (see 1:17). Here we are told that the Law was given to us from God *through a channel,* who was His earthly servant Moses. In contrast to that, grace, because it subsists in Christ, comes to us from God in the person of Christ himself. In other words, Christ is not a channel through whom grace—as an entity separate from himself—comes to us; rather, in Christ himself grace subsists. This means that in the present context, this word subsists conveys the thought that grace had its *beginning* in the world with the coming of Christ and grace *continues its existence* in the world in Him.

It is important for us to realize that prior to Jesus' entry into this world there was no such thing as grace upon the earth. As a matter of fact, grace was entirely unknown to mankind upon the earth during that lengthy period. But when the Lord Jesus finally came, He in himself brought grace to this world. Indeed, it was His coming which constituted the very first time that the world had ever known what grace is: even Christ himself. Furthermore, Christ's very coming was the beginning of the presence of grace on the earth, and even its continued existence here subsists also in Christ; for such is His fullness. We know this to be true because John's Gospel additionally informs us that "of Christ's fullness we all have received: grace upon grace upon grace" (see 1:16). Out of Christ's fullness we receive multiplied portions of grace. He himself being grace, He imparts grace; and upon our receiving grace, we ought to be most grateful, and be gracious towards others, even as Christ himself is.

Prior to receiving Christ as Savior and Lord the best we knew regarding living righteously was to follow the principle of the

Mosaic Law which called for our reciprocating "an eye for an eye, a tooth for a tooth," and so on (Exodus 21:23ff.). That appeared to be the highest level of moral justice we could ever arrive at in terms of righteousness. Back then, therefore, our thought was to do our best to try to keep the Law, which at its highest level was the observance of the principle of an eye for an eye, etc., etc. In fact, that principle of the Law, we discovered, was the highest and best level to which keepers of the Law could naturally in and of themselves aspire to observe.

Following our conversion to Christ, however, we learned that grace requires us to walk "the second mile" (see Matthew 5:41). Yet, for us to do such is that which is completely beyond us. Only grace can enable us to go that second mile.

How Grace Is Expressed

You may wonder in what ways does being gracious express itself; that is to say, How is grace expressed? I would like for us to consider a number of ways by which I believe graciousness is expressed.

Forgiveness

As we saw earlier in Jesus' parable of the unmerciful bondslave, to forgive is one expression of being gracious. I believe you will agree with me that it is very difficult for us to forgive. We have in the English language that very familiar saying, "To err is human, to forgive, divine" (a line from a poem by the English poet, Alexander Pope, 1711). In other words, for human beings to forgive is impossible: for us to make a mistake, that is quite human since everybody does it; but for us humans, to forgive is that which requires the aid of the Divine. That is most true!

How can we believers in Christ forgive others if we do not recognize how greatly we have been forgiven by God? A person who has never appreciated how much he or she has been forgiven will never be moved to forgive others. Oh, how gracious God has been towards us in having forgiven us of our sins and transgressions! We, as it were, owed Him ten million dollars, and

He forgave us that debt totally. How, then, can we be so ungracious to withhold forgiveness towards our brother or sister who may owe us merely twenty dollars? We must learn to forgive, which is an expression of being gracious.

In this connection, one basic principle which ought to guide us here is the following: we should demand righteousness of ourselves, but towards others we should extend grace. Too often this principle gets reversed in our relationship with others: we demand righteousness of others but we are most gracious towards ourselves, we excusing ourselves much of the time in being very kind, gentle and gracious towards ourselves but very strict in demanding righteousness of others. And in defense of our position we say to ourselves, "Well, we are simply being righteous; is that not correct?" In response, I would say, "Yes, that is correct, but where is the touch of grace?" For as one wise and gracious saying in the book of Proverbs asserts: "Good sense [or, discretion, ASV] makes a man slow to anger [or, gives him patience, NIV], and it is his glory to overlook [or, pass over, ASV] an offense" (19:11 RSV).

We need to be righteous towards ourselves, not excusing ourselves all the time; otherwise, we will become quite careless and loose, with no character development taking place within us. We must insist on demanding righteousness of ourselves in all matters—even in small ones. We too often have the attitude, "This thing I have done is such a minor infraction of righteous conduct, and hence, it does not matter." On the contrary, it does matter a great deal. We must be strict in requiring of ourselves that we conduct ourselves very righteously; but with others, we need to extend grace where appropriate and not be that demanding; indeed, we need to forgive instead.

Do realize that if you do not learn to forgive, you will become hardened. It is in forgiving others that your heart is enlarged and softened. Moreover, when you forgive a person, you yourself gain more than the person forgiven. Do not harbor in your mind the idea that because you forgive, you suffer loss—you supposing, for example, that if a person owes you a dollar you will lose that dollar should you forgive that person. Do not reason along that line but realize instead that your heart will be enlarged and expanded somewhat each time by your extending grace in forgiving that person. The gain of an enlarged heart cannot be measured in terms of the loss of money or possessions, for if you fail to forgive, you gain not an expanded and softened heart but a hardened heart. This is why it was necessary for the Lord Jesus to teach His disciples the following: "If you fail to forgive from your heart the sins of your brethren, neither will your heavenly Father forgive you your sins" (see Matthew 18:35 with 6:15). And why? Because you have not a softened heart but a hardened heart.

One distinct impression which I believe we shall be left with when reading through the New Testament is this: the spirit of Christ is the spirit of forgiving. How often, in fact, we are told in those same Scriptures of our need to forgive one another. Oh, how necessary to be manifested is this forgiving spirit, especially when we are together as members one of another in the body of Christ: there needs to be much forgiving taking place in the assembly of God's people. In fact, in some of the apostle Paul's epistles we find him exhorting the saints by writing: "forgiving one another" or "forbearing and forgiving one another" (see, e.g., Ephesians 4:32, Colossians 3:13). Otherwise, there is no way "to keep the unity of the Spirit in the uniting bond of peace" among God's people (Ephesians 4:3), and thus no way to build up one another. Let us therefore learn to be gracious in forgiving one another in the church of God.

Kindness

Another expression of being gracious is showing kindness. Indeed, several of the proverbs quoted at the outset of this message today reflects the truth of this statement. For let us notice that though the word kindness only appears once among those quoted sayings (19:22), three others, though employing the word gracious, nonetheless convey the thought of kindness being shown: "he that is gracious to the afflicted" (14:21); "he [who] is gracious to the needy" (14:31); and "he that is gracious to the poor" (19:17). Moreover, it is particularly instructive to take note of what Paul states in his first epistle to the Corinthian church regarding the relationship of kindness to love: "Love suffereth long and is kind" (13:4a ASV).

Love not only suffers lengthily but is also kind. With respect to the first reaction called for by love, suppose someone treats you badly and continues to do so. Love requires you to endure it rather than push back according to the best of the Law's "eye for an eye" principle of justice. You are willing to suffer and endure and forbear. So far, that is very good on your part, for that is the first requirement of love's manifestation, which is passive in nature. However, love is also kind, calling for you to respond actively with kindness: when someone treats you evilly, you repay with goodness. That is kindness, and that is an expression of graciousness.

Furthermore, suppose someone looks at you and gives you an evil eye. What are you to do? Well, there are four different responses for you to choose from. One response would be what is usually done by fallen man, which is for you to return the evil eye with two evil glances of your own, and that would be considered to be unrighteous conduct on your part. A second possible response would be for you to return the evil eye with but one evil glance of your own, and that would be manifesting righteousness according to the Law's justice principle of "an eye for an eye." If, on the other hand, you look back not at all, which is a third kind of response at your disposal, that is deemed by Paul's initial definition of love to be your willingness to passively endure and suffer patiently. However, if, fourthly, you are willing to do that which is over, above and beyond even that third response, it would be actively showing kindness on your part. And what would that fourth kind of response be? You return the person's evil eye with a genuine innocent smile. That not only would be deemed to be kindness, it would also be considered to be an expression of graciousness.

Let us take note of Jesus' kindness He had shown His betrayer, Judas Iscariot, at the time of the Lord's last Passover supper with His disciples. And to better understand how the Lord Jesus manifested His kindness towards Judas, I must explain one particular Jewish custom in that day which figured prominently in Jesus' kindness shown Judas. The way an honored guest at a meal or feast would be treated by the host would be for the latter to dip a morsel of food, usually bread, into a bowl of soup, broth, sauce, or gravy of some kind and offer it to the guest, and it would be given, as one Bible commentator has noted, "in token of special favor and friendship."

And so, at a certain moment at the start of the Passover feast, Jesus—"greatly troubled in spirit"—testified openly that one of the Twelve would betray Him. And in response to the disciple John's inquiry of Him as to that person's identity, the Lord simply but inexplicably said, by way of kindness towards Judas, that "to whom I give the morsel, that will be the one to betray Me." However, though Jesus indeed gave the sop to Judas, the other disciples knew not that it was he who would betray their Master. And why? Because the Lord's noble-like gesture in extending to Judas the sign of his being the honored guest that evening was so opposite, so incongruous, so incompatible in nature in relation to the announcement by Jesus that one of them was going to betray Him. And hence, the other disciples—knowing that Judas was their treasurer—incorrectly thought Jesus' dismissal of Judas from the feast with the words, "What thou doest, do quickly," had reference to a desire by Jesus for Judas to make further purchases for their feasting together or else for him to give some funds to the poor.

Consequently, by not identifying and humiliating His betrayer by name in the presence of Judas's fellow disciples, Jesus manifested an expression of great kindness towards His betrayer. Thus, all which Jesus did that evening in relation to His betrayer was the utmost expression of love and kindness (John 13:21-30). Indeed, it was graciousness of the highest kind.

We all ought to learn to be kind one to another: not only to suffer and endure, but also to be kind.

Generosity

Yet another expression of graciousness is in our being generous and liberal in sharing with others in need what God has blessed us with. We ought to be strict and stingy towards ourselves but be generous towards others. As Proverbs 11:25 (Darby mgn) indicates, we should be "blessing souls" who liberally "watereth" others with what they need. Similarly, Proverbs elsewhere declares that the person with "a bountiful eye ... giveth of his bread to the poor" (22:9). Generosity is therefore a beautiful expression of graciousness.

Gentleness

Finally, gentleness is a further expression of graciousness. The book of Proverbs teaches us that "gentleness of [the] tongue" is comparable to "a tree of life" (15:4). Gentleness can especially be shown by how we use our tongue. On the other hand, our tongue can be very biting in their effect upon others. Should we manifest a sharp tongue we tend not to be gracious persons; for we can hurt people with such an undisciplined tongue. On the other hand, if our tongue be gentle, that is truly an expression of graciousness.

How We Can Be Gracious

How can we be gracious? For as was observed at the very beginning of our consideration together today of this fifth Pillar of Wisdom called Graciousness, we must acknowledge that this attribute or trait is not an aspect of fallen mankind's character. It is simply not in us; in fact, we have not known what graciousness is. Nevertheless, we who are today believers in Jesus Christ can thank God that its potential in embryonic form is currently within us.

Before we knew the Lord Jesus, grace was something unknown and totally foreign to us: the best we could ever hope to achieve—and *that,* by our own effort—was the keeping of the Law. But by our having come to know the Lord and having received His life into us, grace's potentiality is today in us. Yet, though it be in us, we must recognize and ever acknowledge that the outworking of grace in its expression cannot be the result of any effort on our part but graciousness is only to be found in Christ. This is because the life of Christ in us is none other than a life of graciousness. Indeed, it cannot be a life of *un*graciousness, simply because the very nature of Christ is that of graciousness. And hence, since the life of Christ in us is in part characterized by being gracious, all we need do is to allow that life to flow forth from us; and then we, too, will be gracious.

However, trouble arises, in that whenever we hear that we ought to be gracious, we immediately attempt to be gracious by ourselves—that is, by our own effort. By so doing, though, we place ourselves under bondage to the Law; for in our trying to be gracious, we discover we cannot be so; and since we cannot be gracious, we come under the condemnation of the Law and are therefore no longer in freedom but in bondage to the Law (Romans 7).

That is not the way which God desires for you to live out the Christ-life. God's summation, as it were, of your situation is as follows:

> "True, you are unable to be gracious, and I well know it. Please understand that I have never asked *you* to be gracious; rather, I am, as it were, asking myself in the Person of My Son who is in you to be gracious. For even as My servant Paul has written: 'You have been crucified with Christ, and you therefore no longer live but Christ lives in you; and even the life you now live in the flesh you are to live by faith in My Son who has loved you and given himself up for you'" (see Galatians 2:20).

Now that is the secret for being gracious. We realize we ought to be gracious, and we therefore try to be so, but it seems as though we always have to try before we learn the secret.

Suppose a brother or sister in the church treats us badly. We readily acknowledge that we should be gracious towards that person in response, but what usually happens is that we struggle over the matter and attempt to be gracious, but we are unable to be so. We may even outwardly appear to be gracious; inwardly, however, it is another story, and we well know it. No matter how much we try, genuine graciousness does not come forth from us because it is simply not in us. Regardless how great the attempt, we cannot produce graciousness.

Thank God that we have Christ in us who is full of grace which has been proven and tested to be true. For when Christ walked upon the earth, He had exhibited that graciousness fully time after time. And the potential of that same graciousness is within us, but our problem continues to be, how can that potential of His grace be brought out from us? There is a process through which the gracious life of Christ in us can be brought forth from us. That process, briefly stated, is the cross: it is through death and resurrection, and there is no other way. When we are faced with a situation in which we should be gracious and yet we cannot, what should be the solution? The solution is for us to go through the process of dying.

We know within ourselves that we should be gracious, nonetheless we find we cannot. At times the truth of this will be manifested outwardly, and at other times we manage to keep it within us. Yet, the substance of that truth is the same: we cannot be gracious because there is no graciousness within us. We therefore cry out to the Lord, "Lord, graciousness is not in me, I am unable to be gracious in this situation." What is happening? We are experiencing the process of dying. What characterizes this dying? It is having the feeling of utter weakness, a sense of utter inability to do what is required of us of extending graciousness; and *that* is very humiliating: to have to acknowledge the fact that having tried to be gracious we had to admit to ourselves that we could not do so. And in going through this process of dying, we arrive at a point in which we must confess to the Lord: "Lord, I am finished; I cannot be gracious. Not only am I unable, I am no longer going to try to be so, for I now realize it is useless to even try anymore."

Now that sounds extremely bad and quite defeatist; nevertheless, thank God that we have arrived at that very point of giving up on ourselves and acknowledging: "Lord, I give up on myself and give myself to You; for if You want me to be gracious, You will have to be that grace in me and extend graciousness through me: I am depending on You, Lord, to perform it." And as we cast ourselves upon the Lord, He will take us up and express His graciousness through us.

Moreover, to our surprise we will now be able to be gracious in situations which we were unable to be so before. But let us never forget that such graciousness which now comes forth from us is not of ourselves but that it is Christ in us who is the One being gracious to people. It is for this reason that there is nothing of which we can boast. There is always the temptation that after we have extended graciousness to others we may think, "Oh, I am very gracious." No, we cannot take pride in what has occurred; rather, we must always remind ourselves that it is not us but it is Christ in and through us. We have to give the glory to Him. Otherwise, if we become so foolish as to think that we in ourselves possess this graciousness, we shall soon encounter a test whereby we must experience afresh the realization that grace is not in us.

Furthermore, in order that this character-trait of graciousness in the Christ-life can be developed and fully matured in you, you must continue to go through the painful process of death and resurrection; or as the apostle Paul has described this process:

> ... always bearing about in the body the dying of Jesus, that the life also of Jesus may be manifested in our body; for we who live are always delivered unto death on account of Jesus, [so] that the life also of Jesus may be manifested in our mortal flesh; so that death works in us, but life in you (II Corinthians 4:10-12).

Moreover, this reproduction in you of this character-trait of grace is not that which can be accomplished in a single day. It requires time to fully establish it in you. It requires a period of time for you to deny the old self and to take up the cross repeatedly (Luke 9:23-24).

Please be reminded that to be gracious is painful and means that you will need to lose your self-life, which is thus your cross. Indeed, if you are looking for a cross to bear, it is right here and now. Do not forsake this cross and go elsewhere to find some other cross to bear. Take up this cross here and follow the Lord. And as you habituate yourself to follow Him daily, you shall gradually discover that to be gracious is not a loss but a tremendous gain: it enlarges your heart, gives you joy, peace, health of mind and body, and the quickening of life. In short, to be gracious is good spiritual medicine.

This, then, constitutes the erection of yet another Pillar of Wisdom which Christ wishes to build up fully in us as a strong support of God's House of Rest and Peace which the Lord Jesus is constructing for His Father. And by way of conclusion, let me state again that none of us is naturally gracious. Let us not harbor the notion in our minds that we are more gracious than other Christian brethren. Not so! Whatever graciousness is expressed through us has to have originated from Above, and has to come by way of the process of the cross. It must be the result of our continuously denying our selves and taking up our cross daily and following Christ in order that His life in us may be released—thus "death working in us but life in others."

Oh, how good it would be if, by the grace of God, we can be a gracious people! It would in one sense be almost like what we read in Psalm 133: "Behold, how good and how pleasant for brethren to dwell together in unity!" (v.1) How can we dwell together in unity? By our being gracious one to another. And if that be so, then we shall have the anointing of God upon us as is described further in that same psalm. Moreover, we shall have a refreshing view from Heaven, and the Lord's life will spread far afield on the earth and be abundant.

This is indeed what God by His Spirit wishes to work in us and out from us. May He have His perfect way in each of us—all to His glory.

Our heavenly Father, how we praise and thank Thee that Thou hast put within us a gracious life, a life full of grace. Oh how we praise and thank Thee, Thou hast deposited this life in us, Thou hast given us this potential through Thy Son Jesus. We do thank Thee for that. And now, Father, we do pray that by Thy Holy Spirit Thou wilt lead us into this truth. We pray that Thou wilt enable us to see that this is not ourselves, but this is Christ within us. With man it is impossible, but with God all things are possible. Oh, show us that without Thee we can do nothing, but with Thee all things are possible. Oh, teach us how to let go of ourselves, and let Thee live out Thy life through us. Enable us to deny ourselves, take up our cross and follow the Lord Jesus. Oh Father, we do desire that we may be characterized by graciousness, because Thou thyself art gracious and merciful. Make us truly Thy people, indeed. We just commit one another into Thy loving hand. In the name of our Lord Jesus. Amen.

Pillar 6—The Character-Trait of Discipline

Proverbs 10:17—Keeping instruction is the path to life; but he that forsaketh reproof goeth astray.

Proverbs 11:13—He that goeth about tale-bearing revealeth secrets; but he that is of a faithful spirit concealeth the matter.

Proverbs 13:1—A wise son heareth his father's instruction; but a scorner heareth not rebuke.

Proverbs 13:3—He that guardeth his mouth keepeth his soul; destruction shall be to him that openeth wide his lips.

Proverbs 13:24—He that spareth his rod hateth his son; but he that loveth him chaseneth him betimes.

Proverbs 14:27—The fear of Jehovah is a fountain of life, to turn away from the snares of death.

Proverbs 15:5—A fool despiseth his father's instruction; but he that regardeth reproof becometh prudent.

Proverbs 15:31-33—The ear that heareth the reproof of life shall abide among the wise. He that refuseth instruction despiseth his own soul; but he that heareth reproof getteth sense. The fear of Jehovah is the discipline of wisdom, and before honour goeth humility.

Proverbs 16:20—He that giveth heed to the word shall find good; and whoso confideth in Jehovah, happy is he.

Proverbs 16:32—He that is slow to anger is better than the mighty, and he that ruleth his spirit than he that taketh a city.

Proverbs 17:10—A reproof entereth more deeply into him that hath understanding than a hundred stripes into a fool.

Proverbs 20:30—Wounding stripes purge away evil, and strokes purge the inner parts of the belly.

Proverbs 22:6—Train up a child according to the tenor of his way, and when he is old he will not depart from it.

Proverbs 23:13—Withhold not correction from the child; for if thou beatest him with the rod, he shall not die.

Proverbs 23:17-18—Let not thy heart envy sinners, but be thou in the fear of Jehovah all the day; for surely there is a result, and thine expectation shall not be cut off.

We have now arrived at a consideration together of Wisdom Personified's sixth Pillar of Wisdom of seven which He wishes to carve out and fully establish in support of the House of God's Rest and Peace, which is the church, the body of Christ. And the name I chose to give to this pillar is Discipline. How important that there is such a pillar for what Christ as Wisdom Personified wishes to accomplish for His Father. In fact, the discipline of God's people is most necessary if we are going to be useful to the Lord and to be able to be fitted in together one to another. For as the apostle Peter figuratively observed, when we came to Christ as to a living stone, we became, as it were, living stones as well—having been infused with His very life—for the purpose of being built up together as a spiritual house (I Peter 2:4a, 5a).

Nonetheless, though we have been given Christ's life, there is much of ourselves in us, too, which needs to be removed: much rubbish, many impurities, a lot of rough and rude behavior, and foolishness. Hence, in order for these living stones to be built up together into that spiritual house, there is a need for a great deal of cutting, sawing, trimming, and polishing to take place. And all such necessary activities are works of discipline. Accordingly, we need to look into this subject of discipline quite seriously.

Our Need for Discipline

Now as we open the book of Proverbs, we may wonder what is the purpose of the many wise sayings to be found therein. The answer is actually given at the book's very beginning: "to know wisdom and instruction" (1:2a). Please understand that the wisdom spoken of here is practical, not speculative, wisdom. We read in Psalm 111 that "the fear of Jehovah is the beginning of wisdom" (v. 10a), and that statement has a very practical ring about it. Moreover, in the original Old Testament language the word instruction appearing in the opening verses of Proverbs has also the meaning of correction, warning, and discipline, for discipline is the pathway to obtaining practical wisdom.

As was just now intimated, there are actually two main reasons why we believers need discipline—one negative, the other positive, in nature. Considered negatively, there is much in us which is impure, foolish, and downright full of self: we wish to have our own way and do those things which we like. For we think: "That is true freedom; not only are we free, but such freedom brings us pleasure, joy, and what is so satisfying." Yet, we do not realize how foolish we are. It is because of all the negative aspects of our self-life within us—self-opinion, self-desire, self-possessiveness, self-will, and so forth—that we are in need of discipline for correcting, reproving and warning ourselves; otherwise, if continued unabated, these aspects of our selves would cause us to become wild, uncontrollable, and turn even brutish. Discipline is therefore necessary to purify us and to purge from us all such foolishness and self-centered behavior. That, then, is the negative side to the need of discipline for the Christian.

Let us next consider for a few moments the positive side to our need for discipline, which word also conveys the thought of "child-training." In other words, the divine life which God by His Spirit has put within us believers in Christ requires it to be guided, developed, and to grow into full maturity; and for this to occur, discipline in the form of, and akin to, child-training is going to be necessary. In fact, let us notice what the New Testament book of Hebrews has to say concerning this very subject of child-training:

> You may have forgotten the exhortation in Proverbs which addresses you as with sons:
>
> My son, do not regard lightly the discipline of the Lord, nor faint when you are reproved of Him. For the Lord disciplines him whom He loves, and chastens every son whom He receives (3:11-12).
>
> It is for discipline, therefore, that you must endure, for God the Father deals with you as with sons; for what son is there whom his earthly father does not discipline? … Furthermore, our earthly fathers disciplined us, and we gave them reverence. Shall we not much more submit to the discipline of the Father of our spirits and learn how to live? For they disciplined us for a short time as seemed good to them; but He disciplines us all the time for our good in order that we may be partakers of His divine nature (see 12:5-10 ASV with II Peter 1:4).

Thus, by means of the child-training of our heavenly Father, He is guiding and channeling us as His sons and daughters into matured lives in Christ that will be pleasing and useful in His sight. A person who is never disciplined never grows up. We are therefore greatly in need of discipline if we believers are ever to be built up as God's spiritual house.

Now according to Proverbs it is the fool who despises his father's instruction and has no regard for necessary reproof (15:5). How true that we do not naturally like to be corrected or reproved. This is because there is too much pride in us. However, Proverbs also tells us that if we refuse correction, we are guilty of despising our very own souls (15:32a ASV). And why? Because we are not perfect, and consequently, we are in need of such correction.

Some people like to correct others; that appears to be a mark of human nature. We do not like to be corrected or reproved, and yet we like to reprove others. Even so, the reproofs of those who like to correct others are not of much value. However, Proverbs teaches us that "the reproofs of discipline are the way of life" (6:23b Darby mgn). In other words, discipline will bring us into life—even abundant life. Moreover, there are several very wise sayings in the book of Proverbs cautioning us not to despise the reproof, discipline and instruction of our fathers and mothers; otherwise we become fools (1:7b-9; 15:5, 20; 23:22; 30:17). Furthermore, in applying these same passages in Proverbs spiritually, it can rightly be asserted that fathers and mothers are those who are more mature in the Lord; and because they care about the younger brethren in the Lord, they as spiritual parents are concerned about the spiritual life of the younger ones and at times must minister reproof to them. These younger saints ought therefore hearken to these spiritual parents in the church, since according to some of those same wise sayings in Proverbs this will make them wise.

A Disciplined Body

We need discipline for our bodies' sake. This body that is created by God is meant to glorify Him. The body itself is not evil. Heathen philosophers in the ancient past and other people since then have considered the body to be evil, and because of that they have ill-treated their body physically in order to save themselves. This is not the word of God. Our body is created by Him with the purpose of glorifying God in the body. But because long ago sin entered the world and the body became "the body of sin and of death" (Romans 6:6b, 7:24b), therefore, this body of ours needs discipline. Paul said, "I buffet my body, and lead it captive" (I Corinthians 9:27a). After the fall of man this body with its passions and lusts controlled him. Man lived by the compulsive force of the lusts and the passions of his body. For this reason, we who are redeemed by the Lord must "sternly master" our body and enslave or "bring it into bondage" (Phillips and ASV renderings of I Corinthians 9:27a).

Eating and drinking are legitimate and needed physical activities of our body for it to survive and be maintained. Indeed, there is nothing wrong for us to eat and drink. But one of the signs of the world's last days is that of eating and drinking to excess. For the Bible tells us that just as it was in the days of Noah, so shall it be in the day of the return coming of the Son of man to the earth (Matthew 24:37-39). That day shall be characterized by excessively eating and drinking. There is nothing wrong with needful eating and drinking, but they *can be* a sin if such turn into gluttony, over-indulgence, and the making of these two physical activities as the meaning and purpose of life. For this reason we have to discipline and control our eating and drinking. When Jesus was on the earth, He, of course, ate and drank, but there was no excessiveness on His part. When actions that are normally legitimate but exceed their proper boundary, they become sin.

Sleeping, resting: these, too, are legitimate. Let us not forget that God created night and day. The night is for us to rest, and rest is necessary for us to live. But oversleeping and over-resting can become laziness. And as we saw in the discussion earlier regarding the second Pillar of Wisdom: Diligence, laziness or slothfulness is a sin.

Talking—like eating, drinking, and resting—is a natural activity of the body. And so, God made us with a mouth by which we are able to talk and thus communicate. If we had no mouth, we would not be able to express to others what is in our minds. Hence, there is nothing wrong with talking as long as what we say is right, appropriate, and truthful. But if we indulge in idle talk, in gossiping, backbiting, lying, or talking incessantly, then according to Scripture such self-indulgence is sin. We therefore need discipline in this area of the body's activity as well.

We need to exercise discipline over our body so that our body may be *under* us and not *over* us; so also that the body may be used for the glory of God, and not that we may be used by the body; just as God's word declares that "the body is for the Lord and the Lord is for the body" (see I Corinthians 6:13b). The Christian faith is not asceticism, but it does require discipline and self-control by the Holy Spirit. In fact, one of the "ingredients," so to speak, of the "fruit of the Spirit," as cited by the apostle Paul in his letter to the Galatian believers, is this very ingredient he named as self-control (5:22-23). Yet let us be clear here that the meaning of this term cannot be understood to be that the *self* is in control; for if that were the case, this particular ingredient could not be said to be a part of the fruit of the Holy Spirit. And hence, this term must mean the self *under* control. But under whose control? It must mean that the Holy Spirit is allowed to be in control of the believer's self. And so, for the Spirit to be in control, that means that the exercise of discipline is involved.

Do we know anything of discipline over our body, or are we always yielding to its passions and lusts? (Galatians 5:24; cf. 5:16-17) Sometimes when God is "child-training" us, we may need to do to a *lesser* degree or extent than what the legitimate boundary of an action would allow. For instance, eating has its legitimate boundary, but there may be occasions in which we ought to *fast* for the Lord's sake. If in such a circumstance we do not exercise strict mastery over our body, then we shall not be able to make our body available to God when He might have a special need for it.

Let us recall that occasion when the Lord Jesus was traveling from Judea north to Galilee by way of a walk through Samaria. And recall further that upon reaching the Samaritan city of Sychar, He had become tired, thirsty and hungry. So, coming upon a well outside the city, He sat down by that well to rest and to secure some water to quench His thirst. Now whenever we ourselves are tired, thirsty and hungry, we usually do not even wish to open our mouths to talk to anyone, for we lack the strength to do that.

Yet, when a Samaritan woman from the city came by seeking to secure some water to take to her home, Jesus ignored all His weariness, thirst and hunger, and commenced talking with this woman. He did this in order that He might introduce her to her need of salvation (John 4:3-27). We can see and learn from this episode that the Lord had full control over His body. Discipline was definitely a fully-established trait in Jesus' character when mastery over His body was called for in fulfilling the purpose of God in His life.

Do we, as did Jesus, have mastery over the body? Will our body be able to be given over to the Lord whenever He desires to use it for God's glory? Or will it be the case that should He want to use our body, we find that it cannot respond in a positive way? People who have never known the discipline of their body will be unable to respond positively when God requires its use. If, however, they have brought their body under uncompromising control, they can respond positively when God requires the use of it.

I would repeat that in ordinary days we should eat, drink and rest in a legitimate manner. We should take good care of our body, since it is a temple of God (I Corinthians 3:16, 6:19; II Corinthians 6:16b). Neither should we hurt, harm or over-work our body. On the other hand, we are not to yield control of our body over to it. Yes, we must take care of it for the Lord's sake, but we should never submit to the body's mastery over us. We must be in control of our body so that it may be used for God and His purpose. Only through exacting discipline can this be realized.

Why is it that most of the great servants of God, those who were mightily used by Him throughout the ages, were people who got up early in the morning? It is quite a remarkable fact. There are examples in the Bible, there are also examples of this habit in biographies of those greatly used by God throughout church history: that they were usually early risers. And this fact reveals something about all of them. They all were people who disciplined their lives. They were those who did not love their bed so much that they loved the Lord less. That is discipline's result.

A Disciplined Soul

Our body needs discipline. So does our soul. Our emotion, mind, thought, intellect, will and volition—all these are the various faculties of our soul. But how are they all functioning? Are they driven and used by the self-life in us, or is the self-life being displaced by the Christ-life in us so that the *Lord* can use all these faculties of our soul?

The apostle Paul addressed this matter in his second letter to the Corinthian believers when he declared that the weapons of our spiritual warfare "have divine power to destroy strongholds. We destroy arguments [or, imaginations, reasonings] and every proud obstacle that lifts itself up against the knowledge of God, and take every thought captive to obey Christ" (10:4-5 RSV). If that be true, then you need to ask yourself the following probing questions: How do you find your thought life? Are your thoughts, reasonings, intellectual pursuits, and all the other aspects of your mind's activity really serving God, or do they stand forth as strongholds against the knowledge of God? When you want to meditate upon the word of God, can you successfully meditate, or does your mind begin to wander? Can you think through clearly on the things of God, or do your thoughts become muddy? What about your imaginations: do they fly off wildly without your ability to draw them back, or can you use your power of imagination for the Lord? I'm afraid that too often you shall discover that your reasonings and proud thoughts are set against the knowledge of God. Too often in studying God's word your mind begins to work in trying to put your own thought into His word. Actually there is nothing therein which would warrant your injecting your own thoughts and interpreting it accordingly. Is that in fact the way you read the Bible? Or can the Spirit of God be allowed to take hold of your mind and open up divine understanding to you? You and I must "bring every thought into captivity to the obedience of Christ" (10:5b ASV).

How, though, can this be accomplished? The answer: by means of discipline. If your mind has never been disciplined, if you allow your thoughts to wander, then you will be daydreaming all the time. You will be useless to God, for when He wants you to think, you are unable to think; or when He wants you to stop thinking, you are unable to stop. Without effective discipline our mind is useless to God.

In our discussion today of a disciplined soul we need to consider our emotions and feelings as well, for God wants us to have emotion. Indeed, God himself is full of emotion: He loves the world—that is emotion; He also hates sins; that too is emotion. It is wrong to say that we who are the Lord's should have no emotion at all. For let us consider the Son of man, the Lord Jesus, who was full of emotion while He was on the earth. When He beheld the multitudes all about Him, He was moved with compassion, for they were like sheep without a shepherd (Matthew 9:36). When He saw Jerusalem for the last time, He wept (Luke 19:41).

At this point, then, I need to inquire: Who is using your emotion? Is your emotion using you, or do you have control over your emotion? Are your feelings expressing the emotion of God, or are you merely expressing your own emotion? In this very connection, let us remind ourselves of what the Lord Jesus had strongly declared to His disciples. Said Jesus in so many words: "If you love your father and mother, wife, sons and daughters, brothers and sisters, and, yes, your own life, more than Me, you cannot be, and are not worthy to be, My disciple" (see Matthew 10:37; cf. Luke 14:26).

Now what does all this mean? It does *not* mean that the Lord does not want us to love all those closest to us; nor does it mean that He does not want us to love our own life. Rather, it means this: that if we love the members of our family and our own life so much for self-centered or selfish reasons, that will draw us away from loving Christ. As someone has wisely observed, "Devotion to one's family," and, for that matter, to oneself, "must take second place to devotion to Christ." If love for one's closest relatives and for oneself assumes first place, God will have to purify our love. But once that has been achieved, then we may love the Lord, our family, and even our life *for God's sake*. And how much better *that* love shall henceforth be. Consequently, our soul's faculty of emotion needs to be disciplined. Have any of us ever been dealt with by God in this area?

We must also consider the need for our soul's faculty of volition or will to be disciplined. In this regard, let us take notice of the attitude of the Lord Jesus while agonizing over the cross as He prayed in the Garden of Gethsemane. Jesus prayed to His Father: "My Father, if it be possible, let this cup pass away from me: nevertheless, not as I will, but as thou wilt" (Matthew 26:39 ASV). Do realize that while Christ was on this earth His will was pure and perfect, He desiring to do nothing but His Father's will, just as He had publicly testified to the Jews on one occasion: "I am come down from heaven, not to do mine own will, but the will of him that sent me" (John 6:38 ASV). Though the Lord's will while on earth was pure and perfect, He nonetheless prayed in the Garden: "Not My will but Yours be done, Father." Can the same assessment be said about our will? It is obvious that our fallen will is in great need of purification in order that we may will the will of our Father-God.

I trust, then, that we have come to realize that our volition must express the will of God, that our emotions ought to express the love and compassion of God, and that we should have the mind of Christ. In other words, the self-life in us has to be displaced and Christ's life in us has to be given dominance in our life as we seek to use all the faculties of our soul for God's glory. For His sake we need to have a disciplined soul just as was the case with the Lord Jesus, whose character-trait of discipline in all these areas of His soul was clearly evident throughout His life on the earth.

A Disciplined Spirit

In this matter of discipline we must not leave out of our discussion today our quickened spirit. We may incorrectly assume that the spirit in us is so pure that there is certainly no need of disciplining this part of our human makeup. Yet the Scriptures would say otherwise: "… beloved, let us purify ourselves from every pollution of the flesh and of the spirit" (II Corinthians 7:1). We learn here that not only does our flesh need to be purified but our spirit likewise needs this. Furthermore, another passage of

Scripture indicates the same necessity: "Now the God of peace himself sanctify you wholly: and [that] your whole spirit, and soul, and body be [kept] blameless [until] the coming of our Lord Jesus Christ" (I Thessalonians 5:23). Therefore, even our spirit requires the discipline of purification.

One event in the experience of Jesus and His disciples dramatically points up this very need for our spirit to be purified. It occurred as Jesus was on His way to Jerusalem for the last time with the intent of offering himself up as a sin offering for us all. And on this occasion Jesus had therefore firmly set His face towards Jerusalem and, with His disciples, was currently traveling through Samaria once again. It must be remembered, of course, that the Samaritans were generally hostile towards the Jews. So, upon Jesus and His party entering one of Samaria's villages, the Samaritans there, noticing that the Lord's face was "steadfastly set" on going to Jerusalem, refused to receive this traveling Jewish party for overnight lodging and food.

Now the two disciples James and John—who were the sons of their father Zebedee and known by their behavior as "the Sons of Thunder"—when they observed these villagers' reaction, turned to Jesus and said: "Lord, would You like for us to bid that fire come down from heaven and consume these people, even as our prophet Elijah of old had done? For they deserve nothing but to be destroyed!" We must marvel today at the tremendous faith which these two disciples possessed! These two "Sons of Thunder" were well named, for they believed without any doubt that they could call heaven's fire down upon these non-receptive Samaritans!

However, the Lord Jesus "rebuked them," saying: "You two do not realize what kind of spirit you have." And some ancient Bible authorities have added to this Scripture passage that the Lord went on to say that "the Son of man came not to destroy men's lives but to save them." And so, instead of staying in this particular village Jesus and His party went on to another Samaritan village (Luke 9:51-56 ASV mgn).

What a contrast between the attitude and conduct of the Lord and that of these two sons of Zebedee. For as this party was traveling towards Jerusalem Jesus was manifesting the spirit of the Lamb of God, since He was "steadfastly set" to go there to be offered up on behalf of His disciples and on our behalf today. Yet these disciples of His had manifested the spirit of the world. This reveals, does it not, that not only our body and our soul but also even our spirit is in need of purifying discipline. Since the Holy Spirit dwells in our spirit, our spirit should continually be open in fellowship with the Spirit of God. Regrettably, however, there are times when our "self" will successfully attempt to insinuate itself into our spirit and thus it becomes defiled.

That is why there are times when it becomes necessary for our spirit to be purified. How true the proverb is which declares that "the one who rules over his spirit is mightier than the one who captures a city" (see 16:32b). If you can take a city captive, you are most certainly a very powerful person. Even so, if you are so disciplined that you can control and rule over your spirit, then you are more powerful than the person who takes possession of an entire city. Oh how necessary it is for us to be disciplined in *this* area of our human makeup, too. Unless we are disciplined we cannot grow and we are therefore of little, if any, use to God in fulfilling His will and purpose.

How to Be Disciplined

Having repeatedly been advised in the discussion today that our body, soul, and spirit are in need of discipline if we are to be usable in God our Father's hands, we would naturally raise the question, How are we to be disciplined? Further, Who is the one who disciplines or child-trains us? In answer to this latter question, according to Hebrews 12 it is the heavenly Father who does. Still further, the question arises as to who actually administers the Father's discipline? Is it not the Holy Spirit? According to the Gospel of John chapters 14-16, God the Father has given the Holy Spirit to indwell us; and it is the Spirit who would administer or carry out the Father's discipline upon us according to our individual particular needs. Our Father knows exactly when and where we need to be disciplined, and it is the Holy Spirit who proceeds to arrange all this and administer the discipline accordingly.

We Christians are not like the ascetics of the world who launch forth to discipline themselves. Such people will at times ill-treat their body because they hold to the false notion that the flesh—their body—is evil. And hence, they believe that by whipping, beating and scourging their body, this will drive out the evil which they incorrectly believe resides there; and thus they assume that by this means they shall become sanctified or made holy. All that, however, is heathen philosophy; it is not true Christian faith. God would never want us to be practitioners of this kind of asceticism.

We do thank God that there is One who is all-wise and knows best the when and where—even our Father in heaven. But it is the Holy Spirit who is the One who knows how to administer the necessary discipline upon our lives. And on our part, it is necessary for us to cooperate with the Holy Spirit as He carries out that needful discipline of the Father. How, then, can we have a disciplined life? Or, to put the question slightly differently, How can our life be disciplined so that we may grow spiritually into mature believers and may be useful to God? In response, I would put forward for our consideration the following three actions which need to be undertaken by us if we would have a disciplined life and be useful to God.

1. Be Committed to the Lord Jesus

The first essential action we need to undertake to do is to commit our lives to God the Father's Son, the Lord Jesus Christ. If we have never committed our lives to Him, the Father is not able to discipline us. Let us be aware that there is a very close connection between the words discipline and disciple, the latter of which we become when we commit ourselves to the Lord Jesus as our Master. We will not experience the right discipline if we have not become a disciple of the Lord.

134

Please be advised that the Father will not discipline just anybody. A person does not go out onto the street and begin to child-train all the children there. No, a person will only discipline his own child or children. And the same is true of our heavenly Father. Unless we commit our lives to the Lord Jesus by giving ourselves over to Him as our Master, the Father will never begin to discipline us. In other words, discipline from heaven is only for children who are committed to becoming grown-up sons and daughters by means of the Father's child-training discipline. Consequently, the first essential action on our part is to commit our lives to the Father's Son, and only then can the Father commit himself to disciplining us.

2. Deny Yourself

After we have committed ourselves to the Lord as our Master, we must then, by the act of our will, deny ourselves. This, in fact, is what the Lord Jesus himself said to those twelve men whom He had called to be His disciples. Declared the Lord to them: "If anyone wills to come after Me, let him deny himself, take up his cross daily, and follow Me" (see Luke 9:23). Thus, denying one's self is a matter of our volition: after committing yourself to the Master, you next *will* to deny yourself. That is the attitude we who would be the Lord's "disciplined ones" must have: we must be *willing* to deny our self-life, take up our cross, and follow Him.

3. Be Open to the Spirit's Administration of Discipline

The final essential action you must take if you would have a disciplined life before God is for you to be open to the Holy Spirit's administration of the Father's discipline. You simply need to be receptive to the Spirit's ways of carrying out the Father's discipline as His Administrator. And the Spirit has two main ways. The first of these two is for the Holy Spirit to provide inner enlightenment by means of illuminating you within with a word that is in accordance with the Scriptures. By His speaking to you inwardly you will know and learn to be corrected in your life where necessary for spiritual growth. As God's word advises His people: "Today if you will hear His voice, do not harden your heart" (see Hebrews 3:15). So be open and receptive.

And at other times the Holy Spirit will use a second way of carrying out the Father's discipline: He will arrange your circumstances by raising up certain situations in your life in order to teach you: and when you are surrounded by such circumstances, do be open and make certain you learn what the Spirit is trying to teach you.

By these two ways the Holy Spirit is able to administer the Father's child-training of us unto spiritual growth and maturation. It is true, of course, that when being disciplined by our Father it is not always going to be joyful or pleasant. Indeed, there will be times when it shall be painful or unpleasant. Ultimately, however, through this chastening and disciplining process we shall be made partakers of God's divine nature—even His holiness and righteousness (Hebrews 12:10-11; cf. II Peter 1:4a-b).

In order for the Lord Jesus to build His church, therefore, He must have truly disciplined followers. If we are not those in whom the Christ-life—in terms of His character—is being developed and firmly established through the Father's discipline, we shall not be able to be built up together. How very important it is that there is such a pillar being carved out by Wisdom Personified—even the Pillar of Discipline. And how true, in this connection, is the proverb which would seem to say that if we have understanding when God disciplines us, such reproof shall enter far more deeply into us than would a hundred body blows enter the flesh of a fool (17:10).

It is for that reason that for God to complete His necessary work of discipline in us, we must be open and receptive to the Holy Spirit's administering of it upon our lives. To sum up, the discipline of us believers shall make it possible for Christ to build us together in the church that shall become God's House of Rest and Peace, while at the same time Discipline becomes the sixth strong Pillar of Wisdom in support of that House.

Our heavenly Father, how we praise and thank Thee that Thou hast given us Thy life and Thou hast given us Thy Spirit. Oh, we do praise Thee for the Holy Spirit, who is the Administrator of discipline on Thy behalf. Father, we just commit our lives to Thee. We ask Thee to discipline us, chasten us, and child-train us, so that we may grow up and be built up together unto the praise of Thy glory. Oh Father, do not allow us to be foolish as to despise Thy reproof. But humble us that we may learn to accept Thy discipline. We ask in the precious name of our Lord Jesus. Amen.

Pillar 7—The Character-Trait of Truthfulness

Proverbs 10:9—He that walketh in integrity walketh securely; but he that perverteth his ways shall be known.

Proverbs 11:9—With his mouth a hypocrite destroyeth his neighbour; but through knowledge are the righteous delivered.

Proverbs 12:17—He that uttereth truth sheweth forth righteousness; but a false witness deceit.

Proverbs 12:19—The lip of truth shall be established forever; but a lying tongue is but for a moment.

Proverbs 12:20—Deceit is in the heart of them that devise evil; but to the counsellors of peace is joy.

Proverbs 12:22—Lying lips are an abomination to Jehovah; but they that deal truly are his delight.

Proverbs 14:22—Do they not err that devise evil? but loving-kindness and truth are for those that devise good.

Proverbs 14:25—A true witness delivereth souls; but deceit uttereth lies.

Proverbs 16:6—By loving-kindness and truth iniquity is atoned for; and by the fear of Jehovah men depart from evil.

Proverbs 16:11—The just balance and scales are Jehovah's; all the weights of the bag are his work.

Proverbs 16:28—A false man soweth contention; and a talebearer separateth very friends.

Proverbs 17:4—The evil-doer giveth heed to iniquitous lips; the liar giveth ear to a mischievous tongue.

Proverbs 19:5—A false witness shall not be held innocent, and he that uttereth lies shall not escape.

Proverbs 19:9—A false witness shall not be held innocent, and he that uttereth lies shall perish.

Proverbs 20:17—Bread of falsehood is sweet to a man, but afterwards his mouth shall be filled with gravel.

Proverbs 20:23—Divers weights are an abomination unto Jehovah; and a false balance is not good.

Proverbs 20:28—Mercy and truth preserve the king; and he upholdeth his throne by mercy.

Proverbs 21:28—A lying witness shall perish; and a man that heareth shall speak constantly.

Proverbs 23:23—Buy the truth, and sell it not; wisdom, and instruction, and intelligence.

The God of Truth

Our God is the God of truth: He is the true God and there is none else. For in the prayer of the Lord Jesus to His Father He said: " ... this is the eternal life, that they should know thee, the only true God, and Jesus Christ whom thou hast sent" (John 17:3). What is eternal life? It is to know the only true God and to know Jesus Christ whom He has sent. Moreover, we read in I John these words: "... we know that the Son of God has come, and has given us an understanding that we should know him that is true; and we are in him that is true, in His Son Jesus Christ. He is the true God and eternal life" (5:20). We have been given understanding to know Him who is true, the true God. Not only do we know Him who is true, we also know we are in Him who is true, which is to say that we are in His Son Jesus Christ: indeed, He is the true God and eternal life. Furthermore, the Lord Jesus is elsewhere in Scripture called "the holy, the true" (Revelation 3:7b). And additionally, Christ is referred to as the "Amen, the faithful and true witness" (Revelation 3:14b). And not to be forgotten, Jesus himself declared, "I am the truth" (John 14:6a).

In the days when Jesus was on earth, on one occasion the religious-minded Pharisees, together with the politically-minded Herodians, approached Jesus with the intention of trying to ensnare Him by His own words. So they said to Him: "Teacher, we know that thou art true, and teachest the way of God in truth, and carest not for anyone, for thou regardest not men's person" (Matthew 22:16). Even His enemies acknowledged that Jesus is true, and that He teaches the way of God in truth. Not only that, they also had to acknowledge that He courted no man's favor nor was partial to anybody. In fact, during the whole earthly life of the Lord Jesus, He manifested to all those around Him—both to His foes as well as to His friends—that He is a true man who had no pretense nor falsehood in Him; nor did He even put up any kind of front or façade.

Jesus was not someone who ever tried to court popularity. Jesus proved to all that He was a true man in the perfect sense of that phrase: what He was within is what He precisely manifested without: what He was before God in secret was what He was before men in public. Neither also did Jesus play politics of any sort nor did He engage in any kind of maneuvers to fool people. To sum up, while Jesus was on earth He indisputably stood as the only true and real man in the entire universe. Indeed, that is the impression which the Lord Jesus Christ gave to the whole world.

Now because Jesus was so real and true, He had to suffer for it. As a matter of fact, He was put to death because He was so real and true; for when He was asked the question—"Are you the Son of God?"—He spoke the truth: He said that He is (Matthew 26:63-64; Mark 14:61b-62; Luke 22:70 ASV mgn). And because of that, He was condemned to death by both the Jewish secular and religious leaders together. Moreover, when Jesus was asked by the Roman governor of Judea—"Are you a king?"—He said, "I am born for that very purpose; but My kingdom is not of this world"; and on that account He was put to death (see John 18:33-19:16). The Lord Jesus is true from within and is true without; there is no untruth in Him whatsoever. He is so true and so real.

Then, too, the Holy Spirit is called the "Spirit of truth," who is to "guide" us "into all the truth" (John 14:17a, 15:26a, 16:13a). Apart from the Holy Spirit there is no truth; that is to say, there is no reality. If we want to lay hold of spiritual reality, we will need to be led into an awareness of it by the Spirit of Truth.

The Untrue Old Man

So from all this Biblical description we cannot deny that our God is the God of truth. This is the very character of our God. Since this is His character, He requires of us that we be true and real just as He is true and real. However, a problem arises, in that we are not true nor are we real. In fact, truthfulness is that which is unknown to our fallen, natural man.

Before man sinned, when Adam and Eve were in the Garden of Eden, how real, how true they were! There was no pretense, there was no covering, because there was no need to cover (Genesis 2:25). Yet, immediately after sin entered the world by that first man, the following things happened. First, the man and the woman tried to cover themselves with fig leaves. Second, when they heard the voice of the Lord coming into the Garden, they hid themselves among the trees. Third, when God said— "What have you done?"—immediately Adam began to blame Eve and Eve blamed the serpent (Genesis 3:6-13). They both tried to cover themselves. Ever since that day untruth has been the nature of the fallen old man in each one of us.

Let not any of us believers think that we are very true and very real. No one in the world has been unaffected by the untruth and unreality which came into existence because of the original sin of our ancestral parents. Without any doubt we live in an unreal world, for the whole world is one big lie. And why? Because the whole world is under the rule of the great liar, even Satan. He is a liar, and he rules this world with lies (John 8:44, 12:31, 16:11, II Corinthians 4:4a, I John 5:19). Everything is seemingly nothing but an unending series of mankind's covering-up actions; in fact, pretension is the governing principle of the universe. I would caution ourselves again not to think that we are real and true. No, we are not; for we have lived, and still live, under the great deception of our Enemy: indeed, we have deceived ourselves without actually knowing it; and therefore, we have deceived others. In other words, truth and reality have never been a part of fallen mankind's nature. Accordingly, this means that in our own nature there has never been the attribute of our being true or real. In our fallen and unredeemed state we had been acting all our life and we had not even been aware of it.

When did any of us begin to realize this? It was when the Spirit of Truth began to convict us. Before the Spirit of God convicted us of our sin, and also of righteousness and of judgment (John 16:8 ASV), how did we consider ourselves? We considered ourselves as pretty good! We often would compare ourselves with other people and thought, "Well, now, even though I'm not perfect, I'm better than so and so." Were we true to ourselves? Were we true to God? Were we true to other people? No. We deceived ourselves, not having truly known ourselves. And why? Because we were living under a big lie.

At that time we were part of this world system, but when God's Spirit of Truth began to convict us of our sins, that was the first time we began to face ourselves in reality. We began to see that we were not as perfect or good as we previously had thought. We began to see all our falsehood, lies, pretensions, counterfeits, and coverings. The Spirit of Truth began to tear away all our coverings and we appeared naked before God. And as we appeared naked before Him, for the first time we saw what a sinner we truly were.

It was a great revelation. When that revelation came, it smote us and humiliated us. We did not know that we were that bad. We thought we were much better. Only when the Spirit of Truth brought us to reality by showing us our true situation before God and by tearing us naked before Him did we know for the first time what truth is.

In this matter of salvation it is not how much or how great a sinner you are, for God is able to save the greatest sinner in the world. As a matter of fact, the apostle Paul said he was the chief of sinners (I Timothy 1:15 ASV), and yet he was saved by grace (Ephesians 2:8). But there is one kind of person whom God cannot save, and will not save, and that is a hypocrite. If a person is not honest to himself and to God, if a person is not brought to honesty and truthfulness, if that one continues to be a hypocrite and act hypocritically, then even God cannot save that person.

Why is it that so many people are not saved? There are so many who have heard the gospel, so many who have been brought into a Christian environment and have been educated therein and who have professed to be believers; and yet, they are not saved. Why is this? It is because they play the hypocrite. If, however, they would really be broken down before God and begin to be honest and say, "Oh God, I am a sinner," they would be saved.

The Lord Jesus on one occasion related an interesting and most revealing parable which contrasted the attitude and behavior of a hypocrite and that of an honest and humble sinner. One day, recounted Jesus, two persons entered the Jewish temple to pray. One was a Pharisee, and as he prayed he said the following: "Oh God, I thank You because I am such a good person, not like the rest of men; especially am I not like that fraudulent tax collector behind me back there. I tithe my earnings. I fast twice a week. Oh God, I thank You, and You need to thank me too. I am so good." Even before God this Pharisee was playing the hypocrite; and consequently, he went away unjustified, for God did not hear his prayer. But the tax collector, when he entered the temple, could not bring himself to go forward towards the altar as had the Pharisee but stood afar off. There he beat his breast and said, "Oh God, be merciful to me a sinner. Permit me to be atoned." In other words, as he looked at the sacrifice on the far-off altar at the front, he said, "Lord, allow me to be atoned by that sin sacrifice, because I am truly a great sinner." He was so honest and without any pretense; therefore, he went to his home justified—that is to say, "just-as-if" he had never sinned (Luke 18:9-14).

The True New Man

Now in the light of what has been said earlier today, does it mean that after we have experienced the new birth and thus been regenerated, we now are true and real? In one very important sense that is quite true. We who have believed in the Lord Jesus have been given understanding of Him who is the truth and who is true, and we have been placed in Him who is true. We are thus in Christ who is true, and also He is in us. And because of this, there is truth in us, for Christ by the Spirit dwells in our spirit and we are in Him. We must therefore thank God for the potential which we have within us. For the first time we now possess a life that is true. For the first time we are able to live a true life. But this is only a potential state of truthfulness within us. This is not yet the ultimate of being true and real in our experience.

A key passage in the apostle Paul's letter to the Ephesian believers can be helpful for us here. Immediately prior to penning this particular passage Paul had described in great detail the former unwholesome and unsavory way these Ephesian believers had walked out their life in the world previously. And then, the apostle was moved to continue writing as follows, commencing with the significant word "But":

> But ye have not thus learnt the Christ, if [or, assuming, RSV] ye have heard him and been instructed in him according as the truth is in Jesus; namely your having put off according to the former manner of life the old man which goes on in corruption according to the deceitful lusts; and being renewed in the spirit of your mind; and your having put on the new man, which according to God is created in truthful righteousness and holiness. Wherefore, having put off falsehood, speak truth every one with his neighbor because we are members one of another (4:20-25 Darby mgn).

We who have believed in the Lord Jesus, we who have been born again by the Spirit, we who are redeemed by His precious blood, we who have His life of truth in us, we need to start learning of Christ just as those believers at Ephesus did. In other words, we have the life of Christ in us, and thus there is the potential of our being true and real now. But in order to have that potential in us developed and fully established, we need to learn of Christ continuously. We need to be instructed according to the truth that is in Jesus. This is similar to what the Lord meant when He said, "Take my yoke upon you, and learn of me; for I am meek and lowly in heart: and ye shall find rest unto your souls" (Matthew 11:29 ASV). We have the life of Christ in us and now we need to be continually learning of Him.

Where, though, are we to start in what we need to learn of Christ? It must start in our reckoning by faith that we have a new position before God. This new position has come about as follows: "your having put off according to the former manner of life the old man [or, old self, NASB] which goes on in corruption according to the deceitful lusts" (Ephesians 4:22 Darby mgn). Before we came to the Lord Jesus, we were clothed with our old garment. This old garment is this old self of ours, and this old man or self of ours is continuing to be corrupted through deceitful lusts. Here are all these lusts which are very deceitful, for they seem to offer us satisfaction, pleasure, fullness, and fulfillment. Yet they are deceitful and continue to offer us only further corruption until, if allowed to continue unabated, shall engulf us in complete corruption. This old garment of our old self-life is getting old, dirty, torn, and shaggy; it is corrupted through and through. But thank God, when we came to the Lord Jesus, He not only gave us His life, He also put off from us that old man—that old garment.

In his letter to the Roman believers in Christ Paul explains further concerning our old man. Wrote this apostle of Christ: "knowing this, that our old man has been crucified with [Christ]" (6:6a). When the Lord Jesus was crucified, our old man was crucified with Him. That is to say, He took away from us that old garment and, having nailed it to the cross with himself, He has now replaced it by having put upon us a new garment—the new

146

man, which is created in truthful righteousness and holiness (Ephesians 4:24). The old man is deceitful and false whereas the new man is truthful and very true. This new man is, according to God, created in truthful righteousness and holiness, and we know who this new man is, it is none other than Christ himself. God has removed Adam from off us and has put Christ on us.

All this, God has done, so far as our conduct, behavior, and daily living are concerned. So we need to see that when Christ was crucified, our old man was taken away and has now been replaced with the new man. In other words, not only does Christ live in us: we are also clothed with Christ. Therefore, knowing that this is now our new position in Christ, we are to put off falsehood, and every one of us is to speak truth with our neighbors because we are members one of another (Ephesians 4:25).

How We Can Be True

How, then, can we be true? First, we receive Christ into us as the truth. Then, we acknowledge by faith that our old man has already been taken away, and we have now put on the new man who is Christ. And so, how do we enter into the desired realness and trueness so as to be a true man and thus be real before God and man? For in our former manner of life we had pretended so much and so long that if it were left to us to try to discover where the falsehood is and how we can be true, or if it were left to us to strive to be true, we would discover that we are not able to do that and we would simply fall back into the same old rut of thinking we are being true when actually we are putting on an act.

Thank God, this is not an action which is left up to us to do; rather, it is that which the Spirit of Truth takes upon himself to accomplish: the responsibility of working this change out in our lives is His. All we need to do is say truthfully: "Lord you are in me and I am in You. This is my new position. I refuse to be unreal anymore. I desire to be true. This is my stand because this is what You have brought me to. Now, therefore, by Thy grace I do desire to be real, I do desire to be true, and consequently, I am in Your hands." This is all we need to declare before God. And as we take that stand, the Holy Spirit shall begin to make it all real in our daily life; that is to say, whenever there might arise any falsehood in us, the Holy Spirit will begin to deal with and search out that area. In other words, the Spirit will guide and lead us into all truth. He will search out different areas of our life: those such as our emotion, mind, and will. He will likewise closely review our relationships with other people. The Spirit of Truth will search into every area of our life, and one by one He will tell us where there is falsehood.

The Holy Spirit is thus to be our teacher, even as God's word has made clear:

> ... as for you, the anointing [of the Holy Spirit] which ye received of him abideth in you, and ye need not that any one teach you; but as his anointing teacheth you concerning all things, and is true, and is no lie, and even as it taught you, abide ye in him (I John 2:27 ASV).

Often when we are speaking or thinking or acting or deciding or having some kind of acting or reacting relationship with other people, the Holy Spirit, whose still small voice is within us, shall begin to speak, saying: "This is not true. This has to go. Be real."

Has the Holy Spirit dealt with you in this way? He is trying to remove all the falsehood from you and He is trying to work in you truthfulness, which is a character-trait of Christ. The Christ-life cannot be built up in you if you still linger in falsehood. You have to be true before God, with yourself, and with your brothers and sisters in the church.

It is very difficult to be true. And why? Because it is costly. Let us look into Paul's relationship with the believers in the Corinthian church, especially as it is laid out in his II Corinthians letter. For that letter reveals and exposes this apostle to a very great extent. Now among the believers in the church at Corinth to whom Paul had written that epistle, some of them actually had come to despise, reject, and even speak evilly of him (see chs. 10-13).

Just here, let me pause for a few moments to make the following observation. If you are going to be writing a letter to someone whom you well know misunderstands, despises, and rejects you, dare you expose yourself to them? Dare you tell that person those personal matters which you would prefer remain unspoken? Dare you express openly those things which would cast you in an unfavorable light—those things which might be considered to be indications of weakness and imperfection? More than likely you would instead put forward in your letter to that person your best, strongest, and most flattering presentation of yourself. What, though, do we find in reading this II Corinthians epistle of Paul's?

On the one hand, we discover that because of the troubling situation at Corinth between some believers there and Paul, the apostle felt he was forced to reveal an event in his spiritual life with God which he had kept hidden for fourteen years; namely, that he had experienced having been caught up to the third heaven, even up to paradise (12:1-4). Nobody anywhere had been made privy to this until now.

Most likely, if we had experienced merely the *second* heaven, probably the whole world would have been made aware of it instantly, because we could not wait to let people know of such an extraordinary occurrence. But having experienced the *third* heaven, Paul—being a non-boastful person concerning remarkable spiritual achievements in his new manner of life in Christ—had kept this third-heaven experience a total secret for fourteen long years until, compelled by the force of circumstances in his relationship with these Corinthian believers, he felt it necessary to share it with them (12:11a).

On the other hand, a further revelation of himself made its appearance in this same epistle of Paul's. This had to do with a short period of restlessness which came upon the apostle at the seaport city of Troas. In writing to a church whose members questioned his apostolic authority, this apostle nonetheless unveiled to them the fact that after he had left their midst and traveled to Troas some distance away on the coast of northwest Asia Minor, he had found no rest in his spirit. This restlessness and anxiety came upon him there despite the fact that God had provided a great opportunity there for spreading the gospel; and consequently, Paul left Troas and returned to Europe and into the Roman province of Macedonia.

Here is how the apostle described his personal spiritual state at Troas: "Now when I came to Troas for the gospel of Christ, … a door [having been] opened unto me in the Lord, I had no relief for my spirit, because I found not Titus my brother [there]; but taking my leave of them, I went forth into Macedonia" (2:12-13 ASV). What might some in the church at Corinth who opposed Paul's apostleship have concluded from this self-revelation? They might well have ridiculed him by saying something along the following line: "See, that's Paul for you! –so weak and fragile! Because he could not find a Christian brother of his, his mind had no relief all the time he was at Troas. What a pity. So, he had to leave there even though he left behind a great opportunity to preach the gospel! Where was this man's loyalty to the Lord and to the spread of His glad tidings?!?"

A similar experience awaited Paul when he arrived in Macedonia. Again, here is how the apostle revealed additional insight into his inner personal state: "… when we were come into Macedonia our flesh had no relief, but we were afflicted on every side; without were fightings, within were fears" (7:5 ASV). And the reason for this state of mind in the apostle? It was because he was still awaiting the arrival of news to come by the hand of Titus as to the Corinthian believers' reaction to his previous letter sent to them (7:8a), which most likely refers to what we have as I Corinthians: whether or not they truly accepted his counsel which in that letter had been put forth in strong, even severe, terms at some points.

Hence, Paul was not afraid or ashamed to let these Corinthian brethren think lowly of him. At this point Paul wished himself to be an open book before them; he wanted to be real and true with them; and if what he would share with them would cause them to think of him less favorably than before, that was all right with him; for he himself had even written in this same letter of II Corinthians the following advice: "I don't want anyone to think more highly of me than his experience of me and what he hears of me should warrant" (12:6b Phillips). Paul wanted to be real and true with these Corinthian believers.

We need to ask ourselves, Can we, like this great apostle, afford to be real and true? I am afraid we too often put on a front: we wish to appear so pious, so godly, so spiritual: we are fearful lest others find out the truth about us. And so, we attempt to cover ourselves. In fact, this untruthfulness becomes such a habit in us that not only do we try to cover ourselves before man, even when we come before God it has become so natural a habit to us that we do the same before Him as well! Little wonder, then, that so many prayers of ours are not answered: it is because we are not honest and real before God.

Therefore, in order that we may actually be led into a life that is true and real, God's Spirit of Truth has to deal with our falsehood and unreality. He will need to put His finger on many areas of our life and inform us most seriously: "This here is not true; that there is not real. Be honest!"

In this very context currently before us, we must take another look at Peter. He thought he loved the Lord very much. In fact, he thought his love for Him was most real and substantial. So that when Jesus informed Peter and the other disciples that He was going to be crucified, this disciple declared with great self-confidence regarding his assumed love for the Lord: "Oh Lord, if these other disciples of Yours shall flee away, I certainly will not; I shall die with You, because I love You so much!" Peter thought he was being quite real with himself and with the Lord Jesus. Yet, not many days hence, and in the presence of one simple slave girl, this disciple denied his Master three different times in a matter of minutes. Peter's pretense and self-deception were shattered totally.

There came a morning not long following Jesus' death and resurrection that the Lord had the opportunity to inquire of Peter, "Simon, son of Jonah, do you *agape* love Me?" How did this disciple reply? He now said, with no empty boasting anymore in his words: "Lord, You know I am attached to You, but I cannot say I love You with an absolute love; for I have been found out not having such love as that. I at one time thought I had it, but I did not. You know this about me better than I myself do, that I am merely attached to You."

We can discern here, can we not, that Peter was now being most real and honest. Formerly he had inflated himself as being a spiritual giant—"Lord, I *agape* love You and am willing to die with You"—but was actually being false and under a most serious amount of self-deception. On this latter day, however, and having been greatly deflated in his own estimation of himself, Peter said in simple honesty, "Lord, You know I am attached to You." Peter was now speaking truthfully and now being real. We therefore see spiritual reality in this disicple's demeanor; and because today there is reality in His disciple, the risen Lord and Master responded with, "Feed My lambs; tend My sheep" (John 21:1-4, 12-13, 15-17). The Lord was henceforth willing to commit himself and His work to this disciple of His because there was now truthfulness in Peter.

What Truth Is

All which has been shared thus far today in our fellowship together concerning our need to be real and true before God and man has brought us to the following consideration: There is a great need for God by His Spirit of Truth to be able to develop and fully establish in us His people the Christ-life character-trait of Truthfulness. And, of course, this is the seventh and final Pillar of Wisdom which the Lord Jesus as Wisdom Personified has carved out and is establishing in strong support of God's House of Rest and Peace which is the church, the body of Christ. We have to be truthful and real before our God and our fellow man.

But what is truth? And what does being real mean? Some people assert: "I simply want to be real; therefore, I'll pour out everything concerning myself, with nothing held back." However, to be true and real does not mean for us to be naïve. When both the religious Pharisees and the politically-oriented Herodians came to the Lord Jesus with a question purposefully to entrap

Him by His words, He was said to be true according to these very people's testimony. For let us recall our earlier discussion today of what they had said about Jesus: "We know you are true. You teach the way of God in truth. You are not partial to anyone. Indeed, you do not pretend. We know all this" (Matthew 22:16b). The Lord did not play political or diplomatic games with them and other questioners. On the contrary, Jesus was very tactful, wise, and honest.

Now the question which these two groups of critics had put to the Lord on this particular occasion was this: "Tell us what you think: Is it lawful to give tribute to Caesar or not?" If Jesus had answered that question directly, saying: "Yes, indeed, give to the Roman Caesar," the Pharisees would have declared: "You are an apostate! We acknowledge only one king, Jehovah God!" On the other hand, had Jesus replied to the question with, "Don't give to Caesar," the Herodians would have charged Jesus of being a rebel and revolutionary, for they would have asserted that they only recognized one as king on earth, Caesar.

Let us realize that being truthful does not mean we have to speak forth immediately and directly. The Lord Jesus was very skillful and tactful in knowing what to do or say in difficult or delicate situations in order to avoid unnecessary offense. And in this instance, Jesus asked that He be shown a coin, which His adversaries produced and showed to Him. Whereupon the Lord asked of them: "Now whose image is on the coin?" To which they replied, "Caesar's." And Jesus' response was extremely skillful, wise, and tactful: "So, render to Caesar what is Caesar's and to God what is God's" (Matthew 22:15-22). Like the Lord Jesus, in being true and real we need to be "wise as serpents and harmless as doves" (Matthew 10:16b).

To be truthful and real does not mean that you be rough, rude, or even blunt. That is being foolish. God desires you to be courteous and gentlemanly or gentlewomanly in conduct. To be real and true means that you live as before God all the time; which further means that even when you live before mankind you know you are living before God; which is to say, that there are not two

153

fronts or façades shielding you in your Christian walk on earth. Not so. What you are before mankind is what you are before God, and vice versa. What is within you is that which is without— exterior to you. Indeed, you do not try to make yourself larger or smaller in the eyes of either man or God. Just be yourself before both, and that is what it is to be real and true.

What is required for us to be real? There is but one way and that is to abide in Christ. It is only as we abide in Him that we can be real. Furthermore, to be real, it is only as we walk in the Spirit, because only the Spirit is the Spirit of Truth and Reality. When we are not walking in the Spirit, we are walking in the flesh, and hence, we are unreal: not only what we do or say is unreal, we ourselves are unreal. Our very being is unreal. But if we walk in the Spirit, the Spirit is the Spirit of Reality. It is in that true realm that we can be real to God, to ourselves, and to others.

To be true and real is that which God has to develop and mature in us. It is with truthfulness that the Lord is able to build God's House of Rest and Peace. That is why, in the earlier-quoted Ephesians 4 passage, Paul is found writing: "… having put off falsehood, speak truth every one with his neighbor, because we are members one of another" in the body of Christ (v. 25). Hence, if we cannot be true and real with God, there can be no growth. If we cannot be true and real one to another, there can be no building of ourselves together. If we cannot be true and real before this world, there can be no testimony to the world. May God have mercy upon us all.

Again I must say that to be true and real is costly. It has cost our Lord Jesus His life, and it may cost you your life too. But falsehood is only for a moment whereas truth is eternal. In this very regard, I recall one particular hymn, which is very beautiful and profound. Its wording reads like this:

Truth is often like ascending a guillotine,
Falsehood is frequently like ascending the throne,
But the dead shall mold the future,
And the glorified shall soon disappear.

Furthermore we have God the Father who cares for us in secret; Therefore we ought to be true and faithful in all things.

How true it is that oftentimes falsehood seems to be on the throne. And why so? Because the world is one big lie. Consequently, whoever lies has all the backing of this world; whereas to be true is like ascending a guillotine for having one's head cut off. But the dead shall mold and fashion the future, while the glorified shall soon disappear. But we have God the Father looking after us in secret. We therefore need to be true and faithful in all matters of life.

Our heavenly Father, how we praise and thank Thee that Thou art the true God. Thou art the truth. How we praise and thank Thee that Thy very life in us is the true life. There is no falsehood in it. And, Father, we do desire to live by Thy life. May Thy Holy Spirit deal with us in taking away all the falsehood which belongs to the old man and build up in us the truth that is in Thee. Oh Father, we offer ourselves to Thee. We are Thy workmanship and we invite Thee to perfect Thy work in us so that we, Thy people, may be built up together as a habitation for Thee the only true God. We ask in the precious name of our Lord Jesus. Amen.

PART THREE

Wisdom Beautifies (Chapters 25-31)

Who can find a woman of worth?
for her price is far above rubies.
... She openeth her mouth with wisdom ...
Proverbs 31:10, 26

Proverbs Transcribed

This last part of proverbs begins as follows: "These are also proverbs of Solomon, which the men of Hezekiah king of Judah transcribed." Likewise, in the previous part (chapters 10-24), we were told that they were the proverbs of Solomon. Solomon spoke 3000 proverbs and out of the 3000 we can find a considerable number of them in the middle part of the book of Proverbs. But there were many other proverbs of Solomon which were not recorded.

King Hezekiah began his reign over the nation of Judah some 200 years after Solomon's death. During Hezekiah's reign there was a great spiritual awakening. There were also wise men during the reign of Hezekiah, and they felt led to transcribe more of the proverbs of Solomon. Up to the time of Hezekiah many of Solomon's proverbs had never been transcribed or recorded. Although they were known among the people and were passed on orally from generation to generation, they were never put down into records or other types of writings.

So a number of men of Hezekiah's time began to collect these proverbs, gathered them together, and arranged them in order. That is the meaning of that word, transcribed, which appears in 25:1 of Proverbs. They brought together what had been passed on among the people orally. They gathered them together, set them in order, and then transcribed them. And that is how we have these additional proverbs of King Solomon.

Now the act of transcribing involved more than merely gathering the proverbs together and arranging them in order. That is but a mechanical and technical undertaking. What these wise men of Hezekiah were about the business of doing was more than simply technical in nature. Why do I say this? It is because this activity was the consequence of the spiritual awakening, mentioned a few moments ago. These men had apparently been awakened before the Lord. And so, they took to heart these proverbs which were full of advice, counsel, and warnings which wise King Solomon had spoken more than two centuries earlier.

And in their taking these proverbs seriously into their hearts these words and sayings became their words and sayings. So transcribing Solomon's proverbs was for these men more than simply a mechanical task; it was a serious spiritual exercise, in that Solomon's proverbs became their proverbs.

Wisdom Reproduced

Christ as Wisdom Personified builds God's House upon seven supporting pillars. These seven pillars represent the sevenfold character of the Lord Jesus. By means of the Holy Spirit, Christ's entire character is to be fully developed and matured in us; and then, with us as His building materials Christ builds God's House, which is the church. And with the completion of the building of the House, what shall we find the House to be? It shall be none other than a reproduction of Christ himself.

In other words, Christ as Wisdom Personified, shall have produced himself—His character—in His church, with His church thus reflecting or manifesting His wisdom. For what Christ is, so shall be His church, since His church is none other than Christ himself reflected in us His people. In fact, symbolically speaking, this is why there is a reproduction of the recorded wisdom in Proverbs Part Two being here expressed in Part Three.

For let us notice that as we read through the chapters of this Part Three of Proverbs, there is found to be a nearly identical repetition of what is in Part Two. Further, however, let us take note that within this pervasive repetition there are frequent variations: Part Three's expressed words of wisdom are not exactly the same, word for word, of what had been expressed in Part Two. The thoughts are the same but they are being expressed in slightly different phraseology.

This, I believe, is a symbolic or figurative representation of what we as various and different members of the church of Christ are to be: Christ is in you, Christ is in me, Christ is in all the different members of the body of Christ (I Corinthians 12:12); and yet, every member will probably be expressing Christ in a more or less slightly different manner (I Corinthians 12:27 NASB). We brethren are all here as a reproduction and expression of Christ in His church. All are of Christ; nevertheless, there are variations among us similar to what we see among the parts or members of the human body which obviously are not all the same (I Corinthians 12:14-20). There are various body parts, yet there is but one body (I Corinthians 12:20), and the one body is there to manifest the fullness of the head. So is it to be true of the body of Christ, the church.

Just as Christ is the fullness of God (Colossians 1:19, 2:9), so the church is to be the fullness of Christ her Head (Ephesians 1:22b-23). And this is what Christ desires to see reproduced in His church's members in great variety: He as Head desires to be expressed in fullness through the various different members of His body. And this, symbolically speaking, is what I believe this Part Three of Proverbs represents: Christ as Wisdom Personified is being expressed in a great variety of ways.

The Seven Pillars Reproduced

The many proverbs, sayings and maxims which have been selected from this Part Three of the book of Proverbs and which follow below can clearly serve to illustrate the fact that Part Three is a pervasive repetition—indeed, an oft-recurring echo—of much of what had been expressed in the book's Part Two, but of course marked by frequent variations in the choice of words employed. And as was done in considering Part Two, the various proverbs which follow below have been divided into seven groupings, each serving to identify and describe each of the Seven Pillars of Wisdom—or, as was figuratively presented in Part Two—the seven traits or attributes comprising the sevenfold character of Christ.

Pillar 1: Righteousness (Integrity, Good) vs. Wickedness

" ... take away the wicked from before the king, and his throne shall be established in righteousness" (Proverbs 25:5).

"A troubled fountain, and a defiled well, is a righteous man that giveth way before the wicked" (Proverbs 25:26).

"Better is the poor that walketh in his integrity, than he that is perverse, double in ways, though he be rich" (Proverbs 28:6).

"When the righteous triumph, there is great glory; but when the wicked rise, men conceal themselves" (Proverbs 28:12).

"When the wicked rise, men hide themselves; but when they perish, the righteous increase" (Proverbs 28:28).

"When the righteous increase, the people rejoice; but when the wicked beareth rule, the people mourn" (Proverbs 29:2).

"In the transgression of an evil man there is a snare; but the righteous shall sing and rejoice" (Proverbs 29:6).

"The righteous taketh knowledge of the cause of the poor; the wicked understandeth not knowledge" (Proverbs 29:7).

"An unjust man is an abomination to the righteous; and he that is of upright way is an abomination to the wicked man" (Proverbs 29:27).

Pillar 2: Diligence vs. Slothfulness

"The sluggard saith, There is a fierce lion in the way; a lion in the midst of the streets! As the door turneth upon its hinges, so the sluggard upon his bed. The sluggard burieth his hand in the dish: it wearieth him to bring it again to his mouth. A sluggard is wiser in his own eyes than seven men that answer discreetly" (Proverbs 26:13-16).

"He that tilleth his land shall be satisfied with bread; but he that followeth the worthless shall have poverty enough" (Proverbs 28:19).

Pillar 3: Love vs. Hate

"If thine enemy be hungry, give him bread to eat; and if he be thirsty, give him water to drink: for thou shalt heap coals of fire upon his head, and Jehovah shall reward thee" (Proverbs 25:21-22).

"He that hateth dissembleth with his lips, but he layeth up deceit within him: when his voice is gracious, believe him not, for there are seven abominations in his heart. Though his hatred is covered by dissimulation, his wickedness shall be made manifest in the congregation" (Proverbs 26:24-26).

Pillar 4: Lowliness (Humility) vs. Pride (Haughtiness)

"Put not thyself forward in the presence of the king, and stand not in the place of the great; for better it is that it be said unto thee, Come up hither, than that thou shouldest be put lower in the presence of the prince whom thine eyes see" (Proverbs 25:6-7).

"Boast not thyself of to-morrow, for thou knowest not what a day will bring forth" (Proverbs 27:1).

"The fining-pot is for silver, and the furnace for gold; so let a man be to the mouth that praiseth him" (Proverbs 27:21).

"He that is puffed up in soul exciteth contention; but he that relieth upon Jehovah shall be made fat" (Proverbs 28:25).

"A man's pride bringeth him low; but the humble in spirit shall obtain honour" (Proverbs 29:23).

*Pillar 5: Graciousness (Mercifulness, Gentleness, Liberality)
vs. Cruelty (Anger, Violence)*

"By long forbearing is a ruler persuaded, and a soft tongue breaketh the bone" (Proverbs 25:15).

"He that by usury and unjust gain increaseth his substance gathereth it for him that is gracious to the poor" (Proverbs 28:8).

"He that giveth unto the poor shall not lack; but he that withdraweth his eyes shall have many a curse" (Proverbs 28:27).

*Pillar 6: Discipline (Prudence)
vs. Foolishness (Simplemindedness)*

"He that hath no rule over his own spirit is as a city broken down, without walls" (Proverbs 25:28).

"A whip for the horse, a bridle for the ass, and a rod for the back of fools" (Proverbs 26:3).

"Take his garment that is become surety for another, and hold him in pledge for a strange woman" (Proverbs 27:13).

"Happy is the man that feareth always; but he that hardeneth his heart shall fall into evil" (Proverbs 28:14).

"He that tilleth his land shall be satisfied with bread; but he that followeth the worthless shall have poverty enough" (Proverbs 28:19).

"He that being often reproved hardeneth his neck, shall suddenly be destroyed, and without remedy" (Proverbs 29:1).

"The rod and reproof give wisdom; but the child left to himself bringeth his mother to shame" (Proverbs 29:15).

"Chasten thy son, and he shall give thee rest, and shall give delight unto thy soul" (Proverbs 29:17).

Pillar 7: Truthfulness (Honesty, Faithfulness) vs. Lying (Hypocrisy)

"Clouds and wind without rain, so is a man that boasteth himself of a false gift" (Proverbs 25:14).

"A lying tongue hateth those that are injured by it, and a flattering mouth worketh ruin" (Proverbs 26:28).

"Open rebuke is better than hidden love. Faithful are the wounds of a friend; but the kisses of an enemy are profuse" (Proverbs 27:5-6).

"He that rebuketh a man shall afterwards find more favour than he that flattereth with the tongue" (Proverbs 28: 23).

"A man that flattereth his neighbour spreadeth a net for his steps" (Proverbs 29:5).

"If a ruler hearken to lying words, all his servants are wicked" (Proverbs 29:12).

In all the above-quoted proverbs and wise sayings we can discern a multi-faceted counterpart to what was set forth in Part Two of the book of Proverbs. Figuratively speaking, this multi-faceted counterpart is a reproduction of the character of Wisdom Personified—even the Lord Jesus Christ. And this is what Christ is engaged in accomplishing today in us: a reproducing of His sevenfold character in us who are the members of His body, the church. And when He himself in His character has been fully established in us together, then we as His church shall reflect Him in all His beauty to the watching world. Briefly stated by way of summary, Wisdom in His working beautifies.

Conclusion to the Book of Proverbs

Proverbs 30:1-3—The words of Agur, the son of Jakeh, of Massa ... The man [Agur] saith, I have wearied myself, O God, I have wearied myself, O God, and am consumed [or, and faint, NIV]: For I am more brutish [stupid, NASB] than any man, and have not the understanding of a man; and I have not learned wisdom, neither have I the knowledge of the Holy One (ASV mgn).

Proverbs 31:1—The words of Lemuel, king of Massa, which his mother taught him (ASV mgn).

Before we come to the conclusion of our consideration together on the entire book of Proverbs there are two final chapters of it which deserve some comment because of their remarkable uniqueness. Hence, and bearing in mind the quoted texts above of the opening verses for chapters 30 and 31, we first of all need to inquire who exactly were these two men mentioned here? We are not totally certain who Agur and Lemuel were. Modern-day Bible scholars have generally rejected the Jewish rabbinic tradition which claims that the names of Agur and Lemuel are attributes of King Solomon, or are even symbolic names for him, in an attempt to credit the entire content of the book of Proverbs to wise Solomon. Yet, I do not believe there is any need to accept such a notion but to accept the belief that these two were real individuals who said and did what the Biblical text has recorded about them.

Now with respect to both these men, we are told here that they were Massaites; that is to say, they were of the desert tribe, people, or community of Massa. We learn from Genesis 25:14 and I Chronicles 1:30 that Massa was the seventh of the twelve princes of Ishmael (son of Abraham) and who was the founder of what became over time a nomadic Arabian tribe. This tribe inhabited a desert district called Massa located beyond southeastern Palestine's Promised Land of the Jews out in the desert of northern Arabia as one travels towards Babylonia. Hence, the Massaites were not Israelites but gentile Ishmaelites.

The Queen Mother of Massa

This being the case, then we can correctly conclude that Agur, Lemuel, and the latter's mother—the Queen Mother of Massa—were all Gentiles of the nomadic Ishmaelite community of Massa. Nevertheless, though definitely half-Gentile, their proverbs and other wise sayings—both those of Agur and those of the Queen Mother as recalled and recorded by her son Lemuel—have been collected and included as part of the content of the Jewish Old Testament book of Proverbs. Is that not most marvelous? In this respect, the inclusion of these proverbs belonging to these gentile Ishmaelites into the Hebrew Old Testament is not unlike the book of Job's inclusion. For Job was himself most likely not an Israelite but a gentile desert prince or king who dwelt in the land of Edom outside the pale of Israel; and yet, the book which bears his name had also been made part of the Hebrew Old Testament canon. In fact, the book of Job is considered to be, chronologically speaking, the very first book in the entire Holy Bible.* Thus we have in the Bible this book by a gentile worshiper of God as well as the proverbs and wise sayings both of the gentile Queen Mother of Massa and of the gentile Massaite man Agur.

We thus see here, figuratively speaking, that in building God's House, Wisdom Personified—the Lord Jesus Christ—builds it with both redeemed Jews and Gentiles. Indeed, is this not how Christ has been building the church on the earth these past two millennia? As has been revealed in the Scriptures and as we have

---

* For more concerning the book of Job and Job himself, the reader can consult Stephen Kaung, *The Splendor of His Ways: Seeing the Lord's End in Job* (New York: Christian Fellowship Publishers, 1974).—*The Publishers*

come to realize from our own experience of church life, there are both Jew and Gentile believers who constitute the membership in the body of Christ (I Corinthians 12:13, Ephesians 2:13-18). And illustrative of this truth and reality from Old Testament times, here in the book of Proverbs among untold numbers of the wise sayings of God can be found not only those words of wisdom of the Israelite King Solomon but also those that were taught by the Ishmaelite Queen Mother of Massa and to a lesser extent those wise words of Agur, her fellow Ishmaelite. Even so, God's word also teaches us that in Christ's church there is neither Jew nor Gentile because all therein is of Christ himself (Galatians 3:27-28, Colossians 3:11).

The Words of Agur

Let us take note again of Agur's initial words recorded in chapter 30 of Proverbs:

> ... Agur ... saith, I have wearied myself, O God, I have wearied myself, O God, and am consumed [or, and faint, NIV]: for I am more brutish [stupid, NASB] than any man, and have not the understanding of a man; and I have not learned wisdom, neither have I the knowledge of the Holy One (ASV mgn).

It would appear that Agur was desperately wanting to know God and was diligently seeking and searching after Him; so much so that Agur had wearied himself doing so to the point that he gave up and withdrew from the search, he realizing that he simply did not have the wherewithal to fathom God. For Agur acknowledged that for his finite mind to try to penetrate God's secret was useless, he ultimately admitting that it had worn him out completely. Exhausted to almost having fainted by it all, Agur finally gave up the search. In so many words this man confessed: "I withdrew from my attempt to find God; indeed, I lacked the intelligence to understand Him: He is too far beyond me!" In fact, Agur concluded his confession with these revealing words: "I

168

have not learned wisdom, and neither have I the knowledge of the Holy One."

Nevertheless, despite Agur's despair, he did find God at last. For he prayed to Him as follows:

> Two things do I ask of thee; deny me them not before I die: Remove far from me vanity and lies; neither give me poverty nor riches; feed me with the bread of my daily need: lest I be full and deny thee, and say, Who is Jehovah? or lest I be poor and steal, and outrage [defame, ASV] the name of my God (30:7-9 Darby).

It is evident that this prayer manifests but one primary thought: Agur's heart desire to be close to God that he might glorify Him in his life and bring glory to His name. That was this Gentile man's humble attitude before the Holy One.

Is it not true that the attitude of us believers as members of the church ought always to be like this man Agur's humble attitude? We, too, seek after God; and, oh, how we want to know Him! Yet the more we desire to know God, the more we discover that He is much beyond us. Regardless how much we do know God, there is far, far more about Him yet to know. As a matter of fact, God is a great mystery: we know Him, and yet we do not know Him; for it will require eternity for us to know God more fully; and still we must seek to know God more. Such is the paradox of our Christian faith, but it is the truth.

Now though we acknowledge that we do not fully know God, we can nonetheless be close to Him. We can also glorify Him in our lives, and out of such a close relationship with God there can come forth great wisdom such as was surely true in Agur's relationship over time with the Holy One. For in carefully reading through the remainder of chapter 30 we shall discover that this Ishmaelite worshiper at the feet of Jehovah God uttered many profound words of wisdom which even now remain a mystery to me. Indeed, I do not pretend to be able to interpret chapter 30 fully; because there are numerous things mentioned therein which constitute a mystery to me. There is great wisdom in chapter 30 which even today more than a millennium later we have yet to understand. Even so, is that not true as well concerning the mystery of the church?

The Sayings of King Lemuel
As Taught by the Queen Mother

Chapter 31 of Proverbs contains the words of wisdom which the Queen Mother of Massa had taught her son Lemuel, who later became the King of Massa. What did Lemuel's mother instruct him about? Briefly stated, it was primarily two things: what a king or ruler should be, and, what a queen should be. In other words, what a man should be, and, what a woman should be. By extension still further, what should be expected of a husband, and, what should be expected of a wife.

Rulers, men and husbands should be just, not drink spirits, and should be merciful. They are symbols of justice and mercy. On the other hand, women and wives ought to be diligent and kind, with the kindness extending beyond their own households. They should also be wise.

These descriptions are a perfect picture of Christ and His church. On the one hand, Christ is the king, the man, the husband. He is the very symbol or type of the one who dispenses justice and mercy. On the other hand, the woman serves as a symbol or type of the church as it should be: diligent, kind, and wise. Such, in type and symbol, is the perfect union that God is after: that between Christ and His church.

I would ask ourselves, What is the eternal purpose of God? Is it not the union of Christ and His church? There is such suitability of the woman to the man—as both are described in chapter 31—that together they may fulfill the work and purpose of God on the earth. And such serves as a fitting conclusion to the entire book of Proverbs.

Our heavenly Father, how we praise and thank Thee for Thy word. Thy words are pure. Oh how we praise and thank Thee for Thy word, because by Thy word Thou dost give us Thy Christ. Oh, we do praise and thank Thee. And, Father, we do ask Thee that what Thou hast given us through Thy word may become reality to all of us, so that truly we all may be characterized by the character of Christ himself, that in our union with Thee through Him, we may manifest Thy wisdom—all to the praise of Thy glory. We ask in the name of our Lord Jesus. Amen.

TITLES AVAILABLE
from Christian Fellowship Publishers

By Watchman Nee

Aids to "Revelation"	The Life That Wins
Amazing Grace	The Lord My Portion
Back to the Cross	The Messenger of the Cross
A Balanced Christian Life	The Ministry of God's Word
The Better Covenant	My Spiritual Journey
The Body of Christ: A Reality	The Mystery of Creation
The Character of God's Workman	Powerful According to God
Christ the Sum of All Spiritual Things	Practical Issues of This Life
The Church and the Work – 3 Vols	The Prayer Ministry of the Church
The Church in the Eternal Purpose of God	The Release of the Spirit
"Come, Lord Jesus"	Revive Thy Work
The Communion of the Holy Spirit	The Salvation of the Soul
The Finest of the Wheat – Vol. 1	The Secret of Christian Living
The Finest of the Wheat – Vol. 2	Serve in Spirit
From Faith to Faith	The Spirit of Judgment
From Glory to Glory	The Spirit of the Gospel
Full of Grace and Truth – Vol. 1	The Spirit of Wisdom and Revelation
Full of Grace and Truth – Vol. 2	Spiritual Authority
Gleanings in the Fields of Boaz	Spiritual Discernment
The Glory of His Life	Spiritual Exercise
God's Plan and the Overcomers	Spiritual Knowledge
God's Work	The Spiritual Man
Gospel Dialogue	Spiritual Reality or Obsession
Grace Abounding	Take Heed
Grace for Grace	The Testimony of God
Heart-to-Heart Talks	The Universal Priesthood of Believers
Interpreting Matthew	Whom Shall I Send?
Journeying towards the Spiritual	The Word of the Cross
The King and the Kingdom of Heaven	Worship God
The Latent Power of the Soul	Ye Search the Scriptures
Let Us Pray	

The Basic Lesson Series
Vol. 1 - A Living Sacrifice
Vol. 2 - The Good Confession
Vol. 3 - Assembling Together
Vol. 4 - Not I, But Christ
Vol. 5 - Do All to the Glory of God
Vol. 6 - Love One Another

ORDER FROM: 11515 Allecingie Parkway Richmond, VA 23235
www.c-f-p.com – 804-794-5333

TITLES AVAILABLE
from Christian Fellowship Publishers

By Stephen Kaung

Abiding in God
Acts
"But We See Jesus"—*the Life of the Lord Jesus*
Discipled to Christ—*As Seen in the Life of Simon Peter*
God's Purpose for the Family
Government and Ministry in the Local Church
The Gymnasium of Christ
In the Footsteps of Christ
The Key to "Revelation" – Vol. 1
The Key to "Revelation" – Vol. 2
The Master's Training
Ministering the Word of God
Moses, the Servant of God
New Covenant Living & Ministry
Now We See the Church—*the Life of the Church, the Body of Christ*
Shepherding
The Songs of Degrees—*Meditations on Fifteen Psalms*
The Splendor of His Ways—*Seeing the Lord's End in Job*
Titus

The "God Has Spoken" Series
Seeing Christ in the Old Testament, Part One
Seeing Christ in the Old Testament, Part Two
Seeing Christ in the New Testament

ORDER FROM: 11515 Allecingie Parkway Richmond, VA 23235
www.c-f-p.com – 804-794-5333